MONEY
MANAGEMENT
BASICS

MONEY MANAGEMENT BASICS

Howard Sutton

and the Editors of
Consumer Reports Books

CONSUMER REPORTS BOOKS
A Division of Consumers Union
Yonkers, New York

This book is not intended to be a substitute for financial or other professional advice. If financial or other professional advice or assistance is required, the services of a competent professional should be sought.

Library of Congress Cataloging-in-Publication Data
Sutton, Howard, 1930–
    Money management basics / Howard Sutton and the editors of Consumer
Reports Books.
        p.   cm.
    Includes index.
    ISBN 0-89043-624-X
    1. Finance, Personal—United States.   2. Investments—United States.   I.
Title.
HG179.S87   1993
332.024—dc20   92-46474
                                                                                CIP

Design by GDS/Jeffrey L. Ward
Second printing, September 1993
Manufactured in the United States of America

Money Management Basics is a Consumer Reports Book published by Consumers Union, the nonprofit organization that publishes *Consumer Reports,* the monthly magazine of test reports, product Ratings, and buying guidance. Established in 1936, Consumers Union is chartered under the Not-For-Profit Corporation Law of the State of New York.

The purposes of Consumers Union, as stated in its charter, are to provide consumers with information and counsel on consumer goods and services, to give information on all matters relating to the expenditure of the family income, and to initiate and to cooperate with individual and group efforts seeking to create and maintain decent living standards.

Consumers Union derives its income solely from the sale of *Consumer Reports* and other publications. In addition, expenses of occasional public service efforts may be met, in part, by nonrestrictive, noncommercial contributions, grants, and fees. Consumers Union accepts no advertising or product samples and is not beholden in any way to any commercial interest. Its Ratings and reports are solely for the use of the readers of its publications. Neither the Ratings, nor the reports, nor any Consumers Union publication, including this book, may be used in advertising or for any commercial purpose. Consumers Union will take all steps open to it to prevent such uses of its material, its name, or the name of *Consumer Reports.*

For Selden

Contents

Introduction

You don't need a lot of information to manage your money wisely. You just need *good* information. You need concise, well-focused, real-world information about the key decisions you'll have to face—the ones that can mean saving, losing, or earning large amounts of money.

This book provides how-to and why-to guidance on many important topics. We begin with the idea that risk and reward are related. All investors, and all applicants for a mortgage loan, must confront the question of how much risk they are willing to accept. But regardless of how much risk seems acceptable, there are a number of ways to reduce that risk. These are discussed in some detail.

It's also essential for investors and borrowers to understand how income taxes and chronic inflation will affect their choices. Many investors ignore these factors. They often choose investments that have low returns but are presumed to be safe. But when you calculate the effects of taxes and inflation, the real returns may turn out to be close to zero. We'll show how to make these simple calculations and how to select

1

investments that can be expected to bring satisfactory long-term returns.

We'll talk about why it's important to concentrate on the long term—a span of at least five years. But we'll also talk about why you should have a method of controlling your spending and saving in the short term. This means establishing a practical budget, sticking with it, and making course corrections that fit with your long-term plans. The result of competent budgeting is a steady increase in your net worth—your assets minus your liabilities. We'll show how to calculate your net worth and how to track it over the years.

When it comes to long-term investing, buying a home ranks at the top of the list of viable choices for the average young family. We'll show why investing in a home can be more profitable than investing in stocks or bonds. We'll show how to compute net returns on real estate and how to compare them with the expected returns for alternative investments.

The size of a family's return on investing in a home depends largely on how the purchase is financed. Generally, the lower the down payment, the higher the return—and the higher the risk. We'll show why this is true. We'll also discuss the several factors that affect your return on real estate—leveraging, implicit rent, tax breaks, and the effects of inflation.

Investing in a home usually involves taking on a fairly heavy debt. We'll look at the options for controlling borrowing costs. We'll compare the costs of 30-year mortgages and 15-year mortgages. We'll compare the advantages of fixed-rate mortgages and adjustable-rate mortgages. We'll show you how to shop for mortgages and how to decide when it's time to refinance.

Of course, it's dangerous to put all of your eggs in the real-estate basket. In addition to real estate, your investment portfolio should contain stocks, bonds, and cash equivalents. But for a healthy long-term portfolio return, the bulk of the money you channel into securities should be in corporate stocks. We'll show why.

We'll discuss what university researchers have discovered about the investment process—why investment markets are unpredictable, why professionally managed investment funds tend to underperform the market, why it's important to diversify your holdings, and why a buy-and-hold strategy will lead to better returns than a strategy of trying to anticipate changes in the market.

There's a hard way to invest in securities and an easy way. Many people like the do-it-yourself approach. They like to be active in the securities markets—buying and selling often, conducting their own research, relying on tips from brokers and friends. They like the *game* of investing. But this is the hard way to go about it. It's costly, time-consuming, and hazardous. The chances of your outperforming the market averages over the long run are very small.

The easy way to invest is to buy shares in mutual funds with excellent track records. We'll talk about how you can spot these funds and how you can increase your returns by avoiding funds that have heavy costs. We'll also discuss *index funds*— mutual funds that are designed to imitate the performance of large groups of stocks, such as Standard & Poor's 500 Stock Index.

But you should understand that funds that have excellent records have usually achieved these records either by taking on extra risk or by being lucky in picking the right securities at the right time. And an excellent track record is no guarantee that future performance will be superior.

So the idea of risk remains at the center of the investing process. We'll show why it's difficult to measure risk and why conventional measurements of risk may be misleading. We'll talk about learning to live with risk—about the possibility of thinking of risk as an opportunity instead of a problem. We'll show why your attitude toward risk will affect the way you save, borrow, and invest, and whether you receive small or large returns on your investments.

We'll talk about systematic saving plans. We'll focus on 401(k) and other tax-favored plans. We'll show how a comfortable retirement will depend on how you handle your saving and investing in the years that precede your retirement.

We'll lay out strategies for handling your pension money

and your Social Security benefits. We'll discuss the danger of investing in securities that seem to be safe but are susceptible to the effects of inflation.

Last, we'll explore the opportunities for passing your assets on to your heirs. We'll talk about why you need a will and what a will should contain. We'll talk about estate taxes and ways to reduce them. We'll show how to make sure that your survivors receive your property without complications.

This book is designed to save you time. It will focus on facts, and it will keep things very, very simple. No experience necessary.

— 1 —

The Basics of Financial Planning

Most people are *very* casual about money. They put a small amount of cash into a savings account. They buy some stocks or bonds that a broker or a friend recommended. They buy a house that seems affordable. But they don't really have a plan.

Eventually, when their kids are ready for college, or one of the wage earners is faced with retirement or a career change, it becomes obvious that some serious planning would have paid off.

Of course, there are some real obstacles to serious planning. For one, we're awash in wave after wave of conflicting information and advice. For another, many people think financial planning is boring. But once you understand that many of these decisions can mean saving or earning thousands of dollars, you will be able to approach the decisions systematically.

THE IDEA OF LIQUIDITY

Assets that can be easily turned into cash are considered liquid. Those that are hard to turn into cash are referred to as illiquid.

Generally, but not necessarily, the more liquid an asset is, the less profitable it will be. Since you'll want to keep some of your reserves in the form of liquid assets—for dealing with short-term expenses and emergencies—you should have a fairly clear picture of how various kinds of assets rank in terms of liquidity.

The following shows a loose ranking of several kinds of assets, from the most liquid to the least:

Cash and cash equivalents
   Cash in your pocket
   Checking accounts
   Savings accounts
   Money market deposit accounts
   Money market mutual funds
   Certificates of deposit
   Treasury securities

Stocks and bonds
   Stock mutual funds
   Bond mutual funds
   Stock-and-bond mutual funds
   Corporate stocks
   Corporate bonds

Property other than cash or securities
   Real estate
   Works of art
   Jewelry
   Silverware
   Furniture

Cash Equivalents

Of course, the cash in your pocket is the most liquid asset you have. The money in your checking and savings accounts is close to pocket cash. Cash and cash equivalents—any short-term, interest-paying security—are essentially very liquid.

Stocks and Bonds

These are easy to turn into cash by simply making a phone call. The catch is that prices of these securities rise and fall, and you may be very reluctant to cash them in when the market is low. That makes them moderately liquid.

Real Estate and Personal Property

If you want to sell for a respectable price, it may take time to find the right buyer. And in the case of real estate, there are all kinds of transaction costs—lawyers' fees, banking fees, and miscellaneous closing costs. Because real estate takes so long to sell, it's probably the least liquid asset you'll ever own.

A FEW DEFINITIONS

We'll assume you are familiar with how stocks, bonds, and mutual funds work. But here are a few general definitions:

Stocks

A share of stock is a share in the ownership of a corporation. If the corporation has issued 100 shares and you own one share, you own one hundredth of the corporation. If the corporation is profitable, you may receive dividends in proportion to your share of ownership. But there aren't any guarantees.

Bonds

When you buy a bond, you're really lending money to the organization that issued the bond. The organization agrees to pay off the debt at a specific time and to pay bondholders a specific amount of interest on the face value of the bond, at specific times over the life of the loan. For example, a $10,000 bond that pays 8 percent a year might mature in 30 years. That bond might be bought and sold several times in the interim, and at various prices, but whoever owns the bond at the time would receive the periodic interest payment.

Mutual Funds

A mutual fund is a company that invests in various types of assets—for example, corporate stocks and bonds, government bonds and short-term securities, real estate, or gold. Individual investors can buy shares of the mutual fund, which entitle them to share in the proceeds of whatever the company invests in.

RISK VERSUS REWARD

Generally, risk is related to reward. The more risk you're willing to take, the higher your return is likely to be. But there's no guarantee that a high-risk investment will pay off, and sometimes low-risk investments pay off very well.

Investment risk isn't really very easy to define. For the moment, let's accept the dictionary definition of risk: the chance of loss. No investments are completely free of risk, and some are extremely risky.

Return means the total amount your investment brings you per year. Say you buy a stock for $100 and you sell it for $105 a year later. That's a capital appreciation of 5 percent. And if it also paid a dividend of $5, we say the stock had a 5 percent yield. The total return for that year, then, is 10 percent.

Bond yields are measured somewhat differently. Say you have a bond with a face value of $1,000 and an interest rate of 10 percent. You will receive $100 a year for as long as you own the bond. If you buy the bond for $1,000 and you get an interest payment of $100, your yield is 10 percent. But bonds usually sell at a price that's different from their face value. If you buy this bond for $900, a $100 interest payment would represent a yield of 11 percent—$100 divided by $900. As the price drops, the yield goes up, and vice versa.

By focusing on the *total return*—yield plus capital appreciation—we can compare the performance of different kinds of investments, government securities, stocks, bonds, whatever.

Bankruptcy Risk

The most serious form of risk is what we might call bankruptcy risk. You buy a company's stocks or bonds, then the company goes broke. You may get something back, but not much. Obviously, this kind of risk is more prevalent in new ventures than in large, well-established companies.

Volatility Risk

This is the most conspicuous form of risk. It has to do with the stability of annual return. If a security returns, say, about 5 percent year after year, that's a stable, low-risk investment. But if the return fluctuates wildly—for example, 30 percent one year and *minus* 10 percent the next, that's a very unstable, high-risk investment. Securities that have such extreme fluctuations in value are said to be *volatile*.

What matters is how long you're going to hold a security. If you're going to invest for only a year, you're probably better off with a stable, low-risk security. But if you're going to hold it for perhaps five or 10 years, you may be better off with a volatile, high-risk security. If you can ride out the ups and downs, you may end up with an annual average return of well over 5 percent, and if you choose to sell, you can do so when the price is on the high side. In that sense, you'll receive a higher reward for accepting higher risk.

When you're dealing with securities whose prices fluctuate a lot—from high peaks to low valleys—the trick is to avoid the temptation to sell when the security is in a low period.

Inflation Risk

This is a very subtle form of risk—so subtle, in fact, that most investors tend to ignore it. But it *is* very important.

Let's use Treasury bills as an example. T-bills, as they're called, are short-term loans to the government. Since T-bills are obligations of the U.S. Treasury, which is extremely unlikely to default, there's essentially no bankruptcy risk. And since the terms are quite short, T-bill returns are generally low in comparison with longer-term interest-earning securities.

Historical studies have shown that T-bills have had an average annual return of 3.7 percent and common stocks have had an average annual return of 10.4 percent. That suggests T-bills are safer than stocks.

But when you consider the inflation risk, T-bills don't look so safe. While T-bills were recording a 3.7 percent average return over many years, the consumer price index (the most widely used measure of inflation) was increasing at an annual rate of 3.1 percent. In other words, the purchasing power of the dollars invested in T-bills and other securities declined 3.1 percent per year.

What's the *real* rate of return, then—the rate of return adjusted for the effects of inflation? This is calculated by subtracting the inflation rate (3.1 percent) from the *nominal* rate of return (3.7 percent). In this case, the return nets out to a real rate of only 0.6 percent—practically zero. By contrast, the net return for common stocks would be about 7 percent—much healthier.

Note also that the inflation rate for the last 10 years has been about 4 percent, which makes it even more important to take account of the inflation risk of your investments. The government calculates the current rate of inflation every month, and the latest figures are reported in newspapers, business magazines, and radio and television financial news programs.

A T-bill investor receiving a 0.6 return might shrug and say, "Well, at least I'm ahead of the game." But we can't be sure of this until we make one more calculation.

TAXES

With a few exceptions, the annual return on the securities you own is taxed by federal, state, and local governments. Treasury securities are exempt from state and local taxes, and securities issued by a state or city are exempt from federal taxes. If you want to know how much your investments are providing, you have to account for the effects of taxes.

First, you have to find out what your marginal, or top, federal income tax rate is. This has varied over the years, so it's difficult to calculate the long-term rate. But here's what a married couple filing jointly could expect to pay on their taxable income in 1992:

15 percent on the first $35,800
28 percent on the amount between $35,800 and $86,500
31 percent on income above $86,500

If your family has a taxable income of $40,000, you can assume that you'll be paying 28 percent on the return produced by your investments. (It's more complicated than that, but the 28 percent figure will serve our purposes here.)

Second, you have to add the taxes imposed by your state and local governments. These rates vary from state to state and from city to city. But let's assume that these taxes will amount to 5 percent of your taxable income. That means your combined marginal rate—federal, state, and local—will be 33 percent. If you're in a high marginal tax bracket and live in a high-tax state, your combined marginal rate may be close to 50 percent.

Now let's complete the earlier set of calculations for T-bills and common stocks. Since T-bills are exempt from state and local taxes, we'll use 28 percent as the marginal tax rate in this case. Federal, state, and local tax rates will vary from year to year, but the calculation process will be the same.

Table 1.1 shows how it works out for a single year. When we adjust the return in this example for both inflation and taxes, the T-bills end up with a negative return (the investor is losing money) and the common stocks end up with a modest positive return.

Until you go through calculations like these, you won't be able to determine your real, after-tax return. And you won't know whether you're ahead of the game or behind it. Clearly, some apparently safe investments may not be safe at all.

TABLE 1.1   ADJUSTING RETURNS FOR TAXES AND INFLATION

Marginal tax rates: 28 percent for T-bills, 33 percent for stocks.
(T-bills are not taxable by state and local governments.)

	T-BILLS	STOCKS
Nominal return	3.70%	10.40%
Minus the inflation rate	3.10	3.10
Real return before taxes	0.60%	7.30%
Minus tax on nominal return	1.04	3.43
Net return	−0.44%	3.87%

It's important to understand how taxes and inflation affect
your investment returns. Over the last 65 years, Treasury
bills and corporate stocks have produced average returns of
3.7 percent and 10.4 percent, respectively. In the same
period, the inflation rate has averaged 3.1 percent. To find
out what your real return is, you have to subtract the rate
of inflation from the nominal return on your investment.
Also, since the income from these investments is subject to
income tax, you should calculate how your return is
reduced by the taxes you pay. That is, if you want a realistic
picture, you should calculate the real, after-tax return. Marginal tax rates have varied a great deal. But if we assume a
marginal tax rate of 28 percent for T-bills (which aren't
subject to state or local taxes) and 33 percent for stocks, it's
evident that investors have lost money with T-bills and
received about a 4 percent return on their stocks.

COMPOUNDING YOUR RETURN

It's also important to understand how small differences in
annual returns can add up. If you keep reinvesting your
returns, you'll earn interest (or some other form of return) on
your original return *plus* interest on the interest you've already
earned.

Suppose one person invests $1,000 in securities that earn
3.7 percent a year (the historical average for Treasury bills),
and another person invests the same amount in securities that

earn 10.4 percent a year (the historical average for stocks). Suppose, too, that each investor holds on to the securities for 20 years, replacing any securities that mature and reinvesting all of the proceeds (whether they're in the form of interest or dividends).

Chart 1.1 illustrates what is sometimes called "the miracle of compound interest" (or "the miracle of compound returns"). As you can see, at the end of 20 years, the low-return investment will have finally doubled in value. But the higher-return investment will have doubled at the end of its seventh year. At the end of 20 years, that investment will be worth well over seven times as much as it was in the beginning.

The key idea is that a difference of a few percentage points may seem trivial, but it can produce a huge difference in returns over the long run.

OPPORTUNITY COSTS

An opportunity cost is the cost of choosing one reasonable course of action rather than another reasonable course that might be more profitable. If you take a day off without pay, the opportunity cost is the amount you would otherwise have earned.

Reviewing the example in Chart 1.1, you might choose the low-risk investment simply because it would be more comfortable. In that case, the opportunity cost over a 20-year period would be $4,193.41.

It's not necessarily wrong to choose a comfortable investment, but you should be aware that your comfort may be costly.

SETTING OBJECTIVES

It's never too soon to start thinking about how you're going to manage your income. How much are you going to spend? How much are you going to save?

Americans tend to overspend and undersave. But there's no

This chart illustrates "the miracle of compound returns." It compares a $1,000 investment earning 3.7 percent a year (the historical average for Treasury bills) with a $1,000 investment earning 10.4 percent a year (the historical average for stocks). The example assumes that all dividends and interest are reinvested and maturing securities are replaced with similar securities. After 20 years, the low-return investment will have doubled. But the higher-return investment will be worth *seven times* as much as it was in the beginning.

CHART 1.1   HOW A $1,000 INVESTMENT GROWS AT HIGH AND LOW RATES OF RETURN

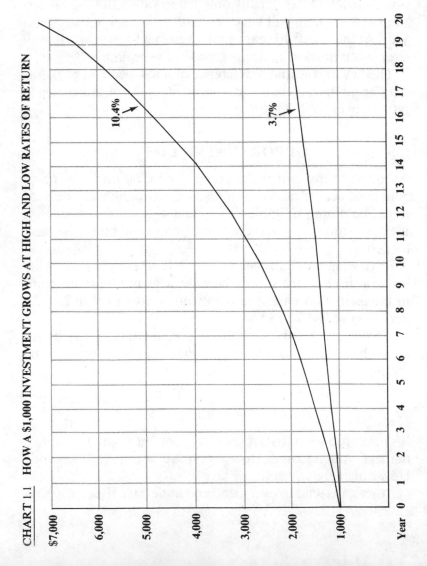

reason you have to follow this pattern. If you establish a steady saving plan when you're young, you'll be amazed how compound interest (or compound returns) can work in your favor.

If you do set up a firm saving plan, you'll have to make a number of decisions about risk and reward. How much risk are you willing to take for a higher return?

As we've already noted, however, risk isn't so easy to define. Many investors tend to concentrate on avoiding risk rather than gaining a satisfactory return. As we discuss your investment alternatives later on, we'll compare the long-run track records. We'll also look at a number of ways to reduce your risk, depending on which kind of investment you choose.

Remember: It's essential to develop a plan—or at least a well-defined point of view that will help guide your decisions—and make adjustments as your income changes.

FIGURING YOUR NET WORTH

One way to chart your progress is to periodically compute your net worth. This is a simple calculation. List all of your assets (everything you own that has some market value), list all of your liabilities (all of your current debts), and indicate the current amount of each item. Then subtract your liabilities from your assets. What's left is your net worth on the date of calculation.

By calculating your net worth at the end of each year, or more often if you prefer, you'll have a series of pictures of your current financial situation. These pictures can be cursory or detailed, but it's important to include the same items every time and to provide a fairly accurate measure of each item's value. Remember that it doesn't matter what you paid for each item; the only thing that matters is what you could sell it for on the date of calculation.

It will be useful to calculate the percentage change (whether gain or loss) from the previous year, which suggests that it would be a good idea to do a calculation every December 31. If you have a computer with a spreadsheet program, it's easy

WORKSHEET 1.1   A SAMPLE NET WORTH FORM

ASSETS	DEC. 31, 1992	DEC. 31, 1993	PERCENT CHANGE SINCE 1992	DEC. 31, 1994	PERCENT CHANGE SINCE 1993
Real estate					
House/apartment					
Other property					
Personal property					
Household furnishings					
Cars/trucks					
Antiques					
Works of art					
Jewelry					
Other property					
Investments					
Mutual funds					
Stocks					
Bonds					
Government securities					
Keogh/IRA plans					
Pension/retirement plans					
Share of a business					
Other investments					
Cash and cash equivalents					
Savings account					
Certificates of deposit					

Money market deposit
   account _____ _____ _____
Cash value of life
   insurance _____ _____ _____
Money owed to you _____ _____ _____
   Total assets _____ _____ _____

LIABILITIES

Loans
   Mortgage _____ _____ _____
   Car _____ _____ _____
   Personal _____ _____ _____
Taxes due _____ _____ _____
Other large obligations _____ _____ _____
   Total liabilities _____ _____ _____

NET WORTH

Total assets _____ _____ _____
Minus total liabilities _____ _____ _____
Equals net worth _____ _____ _____

A net worth statement is simply a summary of all of your assets and all of your liabilities. Your net worth is your assets minus your liabilities.

to set up a net worth sheet that will make the calculations automatically. Then all you have to do is plug in the new numbers once a year.

If you want to make a more precise estimate of your assets, you can include the actual amount of cash you have in your pocket and in your checking account, plus the amount of take-home pay you expect to receive in the course of the month. But this shouldn't vary much from year to year, unless you're in the habit of keeping a lot of cash on hand (which is a big mistake, since it's not earning interest).

Similarly, if you want to make a more precise estimate of your liabilities, you can list all of the current bills that you will have to pay this month. But this figure shouldn't vary a lot unless you've let things slip and have accumulated a huge stack of overdue bills.

The objective is to concentrate on the big items and watch how they change over time.

If you're going to be realistic about managing your money, you'll have to get used to evaluating your spending and saving options in terms of liquidity, risk versus reward, compound returns, tax and inflation consequences, and opportunity costs. You'll also need a firm idea of where you fit in the wide spectrum between the wish to avoid loss and the wish to accumulate wealth. To oversimplify the problem: As someone once said, you have to decide whether you want to sleep well or eat well.

— 2 —

Handling Your Money from Month to Month

Long-range planning begins with short-range questions:

- How much pay do you take home every month?
- How much do you want to save every month?
- How are you going to spend what's left?

Let's begin to answer these questions by examining your pay stub.

YOUR PAY STUB

Federal and state laws require that your employer specify all of your deductions and withholdings on your pay stub. Say you're employed by a company at an annual salary of $40,000, and you are paid every two weeks. Here are the items that would be shown on the two-week stub:

Identification
Name of company, your name, address, Social Security number, and your employee number.

Date of Pay Period
The last day of the two-week pay period.

Total Hours Worked
For example, 70 hours.

Pay Description
The basic two-week salary would be shown as "regular." If you received some extra compensation in that pay period (a bonus or overtime compensation, for example), that would be listed as "other."

Regular Pay
This would come to $1,538.46. Multiply that by 26 (the number of biweekly checks per year) to get the annual salary of $40,000.

Other Pay
If the employee received a bonus of $200, that would be indicated as other pay.

Gross Pay
This would be the regular pay plus the other pay for the two-week period—$1,738.46 in this case.

Taxes Withheld
The stub should indicate how much has been withheld from the gross pay to cover federal, state, and local income taxes. The stub should also indicate how much has been withheld for Social Security tax; this is usually called FICA tax, for Federal Insurance Contributions Act.

Deductions
These are your contributions to various programs. Examples would include a voluntary retirement plan sponsored by the employer, medical insurance, charitable contributions, and loan payments. Since we'll discuss retirement plans again, you might note that these are usually identified by the section

covering them in the U.S. tax code—401(k), generally for employees of for-profit corporations, and 403(b), for employees of certain not-for-profit organizations.

Year-to-Date Summaries
The pay stub should also show how much gross pay you've received since the beginning of the current year, how much has been withheld for various taxes in that period, and how much has been deducted for various programs.

It's a good idea to save your pay stubs for several reasons. You can check to see whether you've had enough withheld for federal income taxes. Multiply the withholding amount on your latest check by 26. If you paid $3,500 last year and for some reason you're paying only $2,500 this year, check with the payroll department. You could end up paying a penalty for not having enough withheld for taxes.

Your pay stubs will come in handy if the Internal Revenue Service (IRS) raises questions about how much you've had withheld during the previous year. Your pay stub will also tell you how much income you have left to spend or save.

BUDGETING

Budgeting isn't much fun, but it can be very helpful. The trick, as always, is to keep it simple.

It probably makes the most sense to prepare an annual budget and then keep monthly records of each item. This will give you a fairly current indicator of whether you're on target.

Start by making a list of a dozen categories of expenses that you'll have to cover in the course of a month. For example:

EXPENSE	CODE
Housing (rent/mortgage)	H
Food/drink at home	F
Utilities	U
Services, professional	S
Insurance	I
Transportation	T

EXPENSE	CODE
Purchases of goods	P
Entertainment/travel	E
Government (taxes)	G
Asset building	A
Miscellaneous	M

Of course, you can organize these items any way you want and call them anything you want. But this list is comprehensive; every bill you pay can be squeezed into this frame of reference.

Notice that asset building, which covers savings and investments, is included as an expense simply because it may be easier to deal with that way. One way to make the saving process easy is to have a certain amount removed from your paycheck by your employer for a retirement plan (see chapter 8). Retirement plans that conform to the government's rules can be very good deals.

The letter codes in our list can be used to make a quick note of each expense you incur during the month. For example, when you pay your phone bill, you can mark the receipt portion with the date of payment and a large U, and throw it into a shoe box. At the end of the month, you can total all the I's, H's, F's, and so on, then record them in a column for that month.

Similarly, you can record daily out-of-pocket expenses, including those you paid with a charge card. If you carry a pocket calendar that shows a week at a time, you can record a cash transaction at the grocery store as, say, F 24.99 on the appropriate date. Then you total all the amounts for each code at the end of the month. The less complicated you make your system, the less trouble you'll have making it work. But if you would feel more comfortable with a more detailed list, you might use the one in Worksheet 2.1.

As mentioned previously, a computer with a spreadsheet program can be very convenient for budgeting. You can also buy personal finance software with budgeting capabilities. You might set up a budget as follows:

WORKSHEET 2.1   EXPANDED LIST OF BUDGET CATEGORIES

HOUSING
Rent/maintenance fee
Mortgage payment

FOOD/DRINK AT HOME
Food
Beverages
Other groceries

UTILITIES
Electricity
Telephone
Gas
Heat
Water and sewer

SERVICES, PROFESSIONAL
Doctor
Dentist
Prescriptions
Lawyer
Accountant
House repairs
Dry cleaning
House cleaning
Day care
Magazines, newspapers
Membership fees
Other

INSURANCE
Life
Homeowner's
Car
Medical
Other

TRANSPORTATION
Gas, repairs
Commuter tickets
Car loan payments

PURCHASES OF GOODS
Clothing
Household furnishings
Appliances
Tools
Other

ENTERTAINMENT/TRAVEL
Restaurants
Vacation expenses
Other

GOVERNMENT COLLECTIONS
Taxes, spouse A
Taxes, spouse B

ASSET BUILDING
Additions to savings
  accounts
Additions to cash
  equivalents
Investment funds—
  mutual, stocks, bonds

MISCELLANEOUS

TABLE 2.1 **SAMPLE MONTHLY BUDGET**

JANUARY EXPENSES

ITEMS	BUDGET	CHECKING ACCOUNT	PAID BY SPOUSE A	PAID BY SPOUSE B	JANUARY TOTAL
Housing	100.00	100.00			100.00
Food/drink at home	100.00		50.00	50.00	100.00
Utilities	100.00	100.00			100.00
Services, professional	100.00		40.00	60.00	100.00
Insurance	100.00	100.00			100.00
Transportation	100.00		60.00	40.00	100.00
Purchases of goods	100.00		25.00	75.00	100.00
Entertainment/travel	100.00		75.00	25.00	100.00
Government (taxes withheld)	100.00		50.00	50.00	100.00
Asset building	100.00	100.00			100.00
Miscellaneous	100.00		50.00	50.00	100.00
Total	1,100.00	400.00	350.00	350.00	1,100.00
CASH PAID IN					
Bank balance at beginning					0.00
Checking account deposits			200.00	200.00	400.00
Paid out of pocket			350.00	350.00	700.00
Total			550.00	550.00	1,100.00
END–OF–MONTH BANK BALANCE					0.00

This is an example of a monthly budget for a two-earner family. In this case, they contribute equal amounts to cover costs. At the end of December, the column totals can be added up for a summary of the year's expenses and cash flow.

In this table, it's assumed that there are two wage earners in the family, with both of them contributing income to a family checking account and both paying some expenses out of pocket. At the end of the month, the contributors can tell who paid how much for what. If they're supposed to contribute 50-50, it will be clear who has paid too much or too little and the account can be settled when convenient. Of course, if one spouse earns more than the other, you might want to split the contributions 60-40, or whatever ratio seems fair.

This form is set up so you can prepare similar grids for all 12 months, and you can have a yearly total at the end. You can buy multicolumn analysis pads for this purpose at a stationery store. Or you can use a computer spreadsheet that will automatically total the figures horizontally and vertically. Using this format, a computer spreadsheet would have two columns for the starting budget, four columns for expenses in each of the 12 months, and four columns for the year-end summary—54 columns in all. But if this seems too complicated, use pencil and paper. What's important is to make a serious effort to analyze your monthly income and expenses and to adjust your outlays accordingly.

You have to be disciplined about recording your expenses (rounding off to the nearest dollar is adequate), and you have to be disciplined about keeping your expenses in line with the original monthly budget. For example, at the end of the month, you might circle those dollar amounts that seem unusually high (in the case of expenses) and those that seem unusually low (in the case of savings and investments).

If you've been spending too much on food, cut back the next month. If you haven't saved enough, make up for it the next month.

SPENDING AND SAVING GUIDELINES

Only you can decide how to divide up your income into spending and saving. But it may be instructive to see how *Consumer Reports* readers said they allocated their income in a 1986 sur-

vey. Times have changed since then, but the general findings
may be relevant. The spending and saving categories in Table
2.2 aren't quite the same as those in our lists of budget categories, but they do show how various income groups handle
their money.

TABLE 2.2   HOW *CONSUMER REPORTS* READERS ALLOCATED
            THEIR INCOME IN 1986

	ALL READERS	$15,000–$30,000 GROUP	$30,000–$50,000 GROUP	$50,000–$150,000 GROUP
Housing	21%	24%	23%	20%
Food/groceries	14	20	15	10
Transportation	9	12	10	7
Entertainment/vacation	5	5	4	5
Insurance/health care	4	5	4	3
Clothing	3	3	3	3
Savings/investments	8	5	8	12
Taxes	26	20	25	29
Other	11	6	8	13
Totals	100	100	100	100

Note: Columns don't necessarily add up to 100 percent because of rounding.
SOURCE: *Consumer Reports,* September 1986

In general, lower-income families spent a larger percentage
of their income for the basics of food and housing. Higher-
income people allocated a larger percentage for saving and
taxes.

AUTOMATIC SAVING PLANS

There are no hard-and-fast rules about how much you should
be saving, but it's probably a good idea to try to save at least
10 percent of your gross income. One way to make it fairly
easy to save is to sign up for automatic transfers of cash to a
saving or investment fund. Here are a few examples:

U.S. Savings Bonds

Many employers will deduct a fixed amount from your paycheck for the purchase of Series EE bonds with face values of between $50 and $5,000. These bonds sell for half of their face value and gradually increase in value until they reach their maturity, though the life of the bond can usually be extended. The rates are usually variable because they're tied to the rates on Treasury securities. You don't have to pay tax on the accrued interest until you cash in the bond. The interest is exempt from state and local taxes. In some cases, where the proceeds are to be used to pay for the owner's or a dependent's education, the interest is also exempt from federal income taxes.

Credit Unions

If your company has a credit union, you may be able to have a fixed amount of your pay deposited in a share-draft account, which is like a savings account.

Retirement Plans

As noted earlier, many employers offer 401(k) or 403(b) investment plans that are financed by automatic payroll deductions. But normally you can't make withdrawals until you leave the company or retire.

Bank-account Transfers

Most banks will arrange to automatically transfer a fixed amount from your checking account to a savings account or a money market deposit account.

Mutual Fund Transfers

If you own shares in a mutual fund, you should be able to have money transferred at regular intervals from your bank account to buy more fund shares.

Buying a House

When you borrow money to buy a house, you'll be paying off your mortgage month by month over many years. As we'll see later, part of each payment will be allocated to interest and part to building your *equity*—your share of ownership in the house. Building your equity is really a forced-saving plan.

CHARGE CARDS

Charge cards make it very easy to spend money. You don't have to carry cash, and the most popular cards are widely accepted by all kinds of commercial establishments—stores, restaurants, airlines, car-rental companies, catalog-sales companies, and on and on.

The trouble is that it's also easy to run up a big balance and big finance charges. What isn't so easy is to figure out how much all of this financial convenience is costing you. Taking a close look at the fees and shopping around for the right card can pay off.

There are three main types of charge cards: credit cards, travel and entertainment (T&E) cards, and debit cards. It's important to understand the differences.

Credit Cards

Visa and MasterCard are the most common. The companies that own these cards handle credit authorizations and collect fees from merchants who are willing to accept the card for transactions with their customers. The controlling companies also contract with banks and other companies (like AT&T) that actually issue the cards.

For the credit card company, there are three sources of income, split various ways between the controlling companies and the issuing companies: (1) annual fees that issuers collect from cardholders, (2) interest that issuers collect on cardholders' unpaid balances, and (3) part of the commissions collected from merchants who accept the cards.

You can't assume that all Visa cards and all MasterCards are the same. It's up to the issuing company (your bank, for example) to decide how much the annual fee will be (some don't charge any fee) and how much the interest rate on outstanding balances should be. Since these fees vary, there are opportunities to save money by choosing a low-cost card. And remember that the interest rates for charge cards are almost always substantially higher than the rates for personal loans from banks.

Sears, which owns the Discover card, offers an incentive in the form of small annual rebates, depending on how much you charge with the card.

What should you look for when you're shopping around? If you're in the habit of paying off your balance every month, the finance charges won't matter and you should look for a card without an annual fee. On the other hand, if you tend to keep a sizable running balance, the interest rate is what you should concentrate on. Obviously, the lower the better.

Travel and Entertainment (T&E) Cards

The most popular T&E cards are issued by American Express, Diners Club, and Carte Blanche. Cardholders pay annual fees that are considerably higher than those for Visa and MasterCard, and cardholders are generally expected to pay the full outstanding balance at the end of each billing period.

Debit Cards

These cards don't involve credit at all. They work more like personal checks. You deposit a certain amount in an account, then draw on that account by using your debit card. You give your card to the merchant at the time you make a purchase and the amount is immediately subtracted, electronically, from the balance in your account.

Shopping Around

There are several things to consider when you're comparing charge cards:

- *Annual fees.* You have to balance this against the interest rates. Some cards have no fee, but a high rate of interest.

You have to estimate what the total cost—fee plus interest—will be during an average year.

- *Interest rates*. You can usually avoid paying interest by
paying your account in full every month. But if you tend
to let part of the balance roll over into the next billing
period, check your card's interest rate carefully. You may
be billed at the rate of, say, 1.5 percent a month for your
unpaid balance. That doesn't sound like much, but it
comes to an annual rate of 18 percent.
- *Grace periods*. Some cards allow a 30-day grace period:
You don't pay interest until a month after your purchase.
Some cards call for an interest charge starting from the
date the merchant notifies the card issuer of the purchase.
In the case of cash advances, interest accrues right from
the date of the transaction.
- *Other benefits*. Card issuers may provide several other
minor benefits. None of these should affect your choice.

Avoiding Trouble

Save all of your charge-card statements. Report any loss of
your card immediately; the appropriate phone number should
be shown on the statement. You're responsible for up to $50
of any fraudulent transactions that occur before you report the
loss. Fraudulent telephone orders are exempt from this rule:
Since the cardholder has no control over those transactions,
there's no obligation to pay anything. Sign your new cards
immediately, and cut up the old ones. Be sure to retrieve your
card after each transaction.

YOUR CREDIT RATING

There are some large companies and hundreds of smaller ones
that are in the business of keeping track of how well individual
consumers pay their bills. These companies are often called
credit bureaus. They are used by lenders to confirm the information supplied by people who apply for loans, charge cards,
and other forms of credit. They usually record your Social

Security number, date of birth, occupation, place of employment, salary, number of years employed, place of residence, number of years you have lived there, bank references, and so on.

Credit bureaus collect information from their subscribers—banks, credit card issuers, and retailers who offer charge accounts. The credit bureaus in turn offer their subscribers reports on individuals who apply for credit. The bureaus check to see how much these people owe and whether they pay their bills on time.

If you're fairly careful about handling your finances, you'll probably accumulate a good credit record over the years. But if you're applying for credit for the first time and don't have a track record, you may encounter some resistance on the part of lenders and credit card issuers. It's also possible that, no matter how careful you are about paying your bills, errors will appear in your credit record.

If you have any questions about your record, ask your bank what credit bureaus might have files on you. Then contact them to see whether they have a file on you.

According to federal law, credit bureaus are required to show you a copy of your report. They don't have to *give* you a copy unless state law requires it, but you can usually get a copy for a fee. And if, because of that report, you've been denied credit within the last 30 days, you're entitled to a free copy.

If you find an error in your credit report, you'll have to take it up with the company (retailer, charge-card issuer, or bank) that supplied the information. If you can prove that there's an error, the Fair Credit Reporting Act requires that it be corrected. Billing errors are also covered by the Fair Credit Billing Act. The time limits vary, but you should have a correction within three months of the time you brought the error to the company's attention. Keep after them.

Creditors do have to correct errors, but they don't have to give you credit. They can't deny you credit on the basis of gender, marital status, color, race, religion, or national origin.

However, they can deny credit if you've supplied inadequate information, if you don't have enough income to be considered creditworthy, if you're already heavily in debt or bankrupt, or if you have an irregular record of employment or residence.

It's important to build a good credit record and to act quickly if you find something wrong.

— 3 —

Where to Put Your Cash

The first question is, How much cash do you need? Obviously, you'll have to have enough cash flowing through your checking account to pay for current expenses—rent, utility bills, loan payments, groceries, and such. You'll also need some cash for unexpected events such as medical emergencies or losing your job.

The rule of thumb used to be that you ought to have enough cash on hand to cover three months' worth of living expenses. That would give you time to rearrange some of your less-liquid investments if necessary. But when the economy is down and the job market is lean, it may be prudent to keep enough cash on hand to cover six months' worth of living expenses.

In any case, you may feel that you want to have a fairly large cash fund just to be safe. But remember that safety is costly. You have to consider other opportunities. You could be earning a higher return if you held that money in the form of a bond or stock mutual fund, for example.

THE BANKING BUSINESS

Banks are in the business of lending other people's money. If you deposit $1,000 in a checking account, the bank can lend most of that money (around $850) to someone else. With other kinds of deposits, such as savings accounts, banks are permitted to lend an even larger proportion.

So the banks' job is to attract deposits by offering certain services or interest, then lend that money out at a higher rate than they paid for it.

Although some checking accounts do pay interest, the main benefit to depositors comes in the form of various services: The bank will keep their cash in a safe place, handle check transactions, and report on the account balance every so often.

Banks attract savings account depositors by paying interest on the amount of money they leave in their accounts. For years the government had a ceiling on savings account interest—5.25 percent for commercial banks and 5.5 percent at savings-and-loan associations (S&Ls). That ceiling has been removed, but interest rates stayed about the same for years. When interest rates in general declined in the early 1990s, the rates for savings accounts dropped, too.

Banks have shifted their emphasis to other forms of deposits, such as money market deposit accounts and certificates of deposit (CDs)—more attractive options because they pay slightly higher rates than savings accounts do.

CASH AND CASH EQUIVALENTS

Checking Accounts

There are so many variations on checking accounts today that it's impossible to consider all of the pluses and minuses. Focus on the key questions: Is the bank insured by the Federal Deposit Insurance Corporation (FDIC)? Does the bank have an office in a place that's convenient for you? How much is the account going to cost per month?

There are three main bases for monthly charges: a flat fee

per month, a minimum-balance discount, and a fee per check. And there are all kinds of combinations of the three.

With the flat-fee arrangement, you pay perhaps $5 or $10 per month. With a minimum-balance arrangement, you pay a fee only if your balance drops under a specific level—for example, $500. With a fee-per-check arrangement, you might pay 25 or 50 cents for every check you write.

What's best for you? If you don't write many checks, you might look for a flat-fee or fee-per-check account. If you write a lot of checks and maintain a fairly large balance during the month, the minimum-balance arrangement might work well. What you need to know is how many checks you write per month and how your account fluctuates during the month. A bank officer can advise you on what your choices are and help you decide which one would be most appropriate.

Savings Accounts

There are two advantages to keeping your cash in a savings account: You will earn some interest, and your money will be readily available. You can fill out a withdrawal slip and hand it to a teller, or you can make a withdrawal through an automatic teller machine (ATM).

Money Market Deposit Accounts

These accounts were designed to offer somewhat higher returns than savings accounts do. Like savings accounts, money market accounts are insured by federal agencies. They differ from savings accounts in a couple of ways. For one thing, there's usually a minimum-balance requirement. For another, because the banks reinvest the deposits in various kinds of short-term securities that are directly or indirectly linked to Treasury securities, the rates on money market deposit accounts fluctuate a great deal. A third point: Depositors are permitted to write up to three checks a month on these deposits.

Although the rates for these deposits are sometimes a couple of points above the rates for savings accounts, that's not always the case. During a recession, for example, the rates on money market deposit accounts may temporarily drop below the rates for savings accounts.

Certificates of Deposit (CDs)

These are really loans that depositors make to the bank. You agree to let the bank use your money for, say, six months, and the bank agrees to pay you a specified amount of interest during that period. The interest rate is tied to the current rates of various money market securities. The interest rate also varies with the length of the loan; the longer the term, the higher the rate.

The advantage of putting your money into CDs is that the rates are typically higher than those for money market deposit accounts. Like deposit accounts, CDs are insured by a government agency.

The main disadvantages are that you must agree to lend a substantial sum and you have to tie up that money for several months or even years. You can withdraw money before the term is up, but there's a big penalty if you do. During a recession, CD rates may decline significantly.

Money Market Mutual Funds

These funds shouldn't be confused with money market deposit accounts, discussed above. Money market deposit accounts are offered by banks and are federally insured. Money market *mutual* funds are administered by private companies that usually offer many different kinds of mutual funds; none of them is federally insured. However, money market mutual funds usually offer higher returns than bank deposit accounts, and they're generally safe.

You invest in these mutual funds by buying shares. The cash accumulated in the funds is invested mainly in large bank certificates of deposit, short-term loans to very creditworthy corporations, and government securities. Your rate of return will depend on the current rates for the underlying securities. Most funds allow you to withdraw money by writing checks, and there's no penalty for withdrawing money at any time.

Some funds invest only in Treasury securities and other federally insured securities. These funds offer maximum safety but a somewhat lower return.

Treasury Bills

Also known as T-bills, these are short-term (three-month, six-month, or one-year) loans to the government. It's possible for individuals to buy these securities directly from the government, but that's not a practical option for most people because Treasury bills have a minimum face value of $10,000. Since the returns on T-bills are the key indicators of short-term interest rates in general, we'll refer to them repeatedly.

How do the rates for cash equivalents compare? Generally, rates for typical cash equivalents—three-month bank CDs, money market deposit accounts, and money market mutual funds—are slightly lower than the rates for Treasury bills.

WHAT'S YOUR REAL RETURN?

Chart 3.1 shows how interest rates for Treasury bills have varied over the last 60 years or so, a period that includes most of the major kinds of events that affect investment returns—war and peace, growth and decline, inflation and deflation.

There is an advantage in taking the long view: While the actual events in this period won't be repeated, the same types of events are likely to occur in the future, though perhaps in a less disturbing way. We may never again experience anything like the Great Depression and World War II, but investors can learn from the performance of different kinds of investments under wildly different circumstances. We'll look at some other long-term charts later on.

The Treasury bill rates show how important it is to think in terms of *real* returns. Both nominal interest rates and real interest rates (nominal rates minus the inflation rates in the same years) are included here, and they offer two very different pictures.

As you can see, there have been a few periods (most recently, the early 1980s) when you could earn a substantial

CHART 3.1   ANNUAL RATES OF RETURN FOR TREASURY BILLS: NOMINAL RETURNS VERSUS REAL RETURNS

The wise investor concentrates on real returns (adjusted for inflation) rather than on nominal returns (not adjusted for inflation). This chart compares real and nominal returns for Treasury bills since 1926. For any particular year, the real return is the nominal return minus the current inflation rate. Real returns were exceptionally high in the early 1980s. But for the entire period, the average real return has been close to zero.

SOURCE: © Ibbotson Associates, *Stocks, Bonds, Bills, and Inflation 1992 Yearbook* (Chicago: Ibbotson Associates). Annual update of work by Roger G. Ibbotson and Rex A. Sinquefield. Used with permission. All rights reserved.

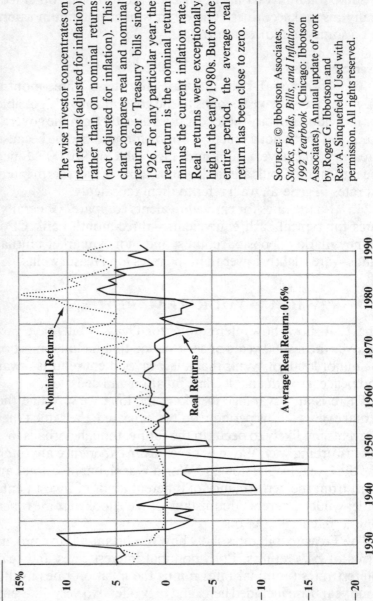

*This chart and others that follow are based on the standard reference work *Stocks, Bonds, Bills, and Inflation Yearbook,* published annually by Ibbotson Associates. The data go back only as far as 1926, because reliable information on investments in earlier years is not available.

real return on T-bills. Most of the time the real return has been small. Over the entire period since 1926, the real return has averaged 0.29 percent. In the 1990s, however, the real return has averaged a little higher.

Remember, though, that this chart ignores the effects of income taxes. If you were to adjust the real returns for taxes, the net return would be close to zero and often negative.

Conclusion: Cash equivalents are a very safe way to hold your reserve funds, but your net return after taxes will probably be modest at best. Cash and cash equivalents are poor substitutes for genuine investments.

— 4 —

Borrowing Money

Borrowing money can be very complicated. There are many factors to consider:

- The *interest rate*
- The *term* (duration) of the loan
- How much the *monthly payment* will be
- The *total cost* (all of the interest you'll pay over the life of the loan)
- The *closing costs* (which you pay in advance)
- Whether you are required to have a certain amount of *income* to be eligible for the loan you want
- Whether the lender requires *collateral* (property that the lender can sell if you default)
- Whether there's a *penalty* for paying off the loan ahead of time
- Whether the interest is *deductible* from your gross income for tax purposes
- How *inflation* might affect the total cost of the loan
- Whether the interest rate is *fixed or variable*

Because there are so many things to consider and so many different deals available, it will certainly pay to shop around and evaluate your options carefully.

CONVENTIONAL FIXED-RATE MORTGAGES

A mortgage loan is probably the most important kind of loan you'll acquire. You'll have to pay a huge amount of interest over the life of the loan, but you can cut your costs dramatically if you pick the right deal.

Since part of your mortgage payments go toward investing in your house, it may be helpful to consider the whole process as a gradual investment, with its own set of risks and rewards. Let's take a look at the basic options and some of the central issues.

Interest Rates

Obviously, the lower the rate, the better. Rates do vary from bank to bank. In fact, in any particular week, in any part of the country, you're likely to find significant differences in local lenders' current rates. The highest and the lowest fixed rate for a 30-year mortgage may vary as much as two points.

Since we're talking about small numbers here—one or two points—it's tempting to think that the difference is trivial. Don't be deceived. A two-point difference is *big*.

Say you have a choice between a $100,000 mortgage at 9 percent and one at 7 percent. In the first case, your monthly payment would be $804.62; in the second, $665.30. That's a $139.32 difference. It works out to $1,671.84 a year, or $50,155.20 for the life of the loan.

Think of it this way: The $139.32 difference is a 17 percent *discount* off the higher price. Even a one-point difference would give you a 9 percent discount. And you get that discount year after year.

Of course, most banks operate in the gap between these extremes. Many adjust their rates to those set by the Federal National Mortgage Association and the Federal Home Loan

Mortgage Corporation (known respectively as Fannie Mae and Freddy Mac). These are federally chartered organizations that establish standards for mortgages and buy mortgages that qualify from banks. Borrowers pay off their loans to the purchasing organization, and banks are free to lend to new borrowers. The advantage for consumers is that this enlarges the pool of money available for mortgage loans.

When you shop for a loan, you'll have to consider two different rates for a particular loan. One is the *contract rate,* and one is the *annual percentage rate (APR).* Your monthly payments will be calculated at the contract rate. The Truth in Lending Act requires that banks (and other lenders) also advise you of the APR.

The APR is based on the interest costs for the life of the loan and includes the points you pay up front. Since the APR refers to *all* of your interest costs, that's the rate to consider when you're comparing loans, if you can get it. But some banks can be remiss about supplying APR information. If they fail to supply it, ask.

The Term

The standard loan used to run for 30 years, but recently lenders have been offering 15-year loans. The rate for the shorter loan is likely to be slightly lower than the rate for the longer loan. There are huge differences in the total payments, however.

Compare, for example, two $100,000 loans, one for 15 years at 8.5 percent and one for 30 years at 9 percent. In the first case, the monthly payment will be $964.74, and in the second, $804.62—a difference of $160.12. Generally, the monthly payment for a 15-year loan will be about 20 or 25 percent more than the payment for a 30-year loan.

But you get an entirely different picture if you stretch the loans out to the end. For the 15-year loan, the payments would total $173,653.20. For the 30-year loan, the total would be $289,663.20. The difference: $116,010.00.

The average mortgage may last only about seven years,

because the borrower sells the property and moves on. But you may have a mortgage for more than seven years, so it's a good idea to confront the term question early in the game: Which is better for you—15 or 30 years? Take the shorter loan if you want to pay off the loan relatively quickly and your budget can handle the higher monthly payments.

But if you want to keep things flexible financially, take the longer loan and double up on your payments whenever you can. That way, you won't have the pressure to come up with the extra cash each month, but you can reduce your total costs. And if you're really disciplined, you can invest the difference in a mutual fund that will earn a respectable income over the years. A $160.12 monthly investment in a stock fund earning 10 percent a year would accumulate to about $57,000 over 15 years.

Monthly Payments

If you want to compare the monthly payments of loans at different rates and different terms, buy a book of monthly mortgage payment tables, also known as *loan amortization tables.* They're produced by several different publishers, and they cost only a few dollars. Some of these books are skimpy. You'll be better served with one that includes tables covering not only whole numbers—for example, 8 percent and 9 percent—but also in-between numbers—8.25, 8.5, and 8.75 percent, for instance. In addition, many books that contain monthly interest payment tables contain tables showing how much of your loan will be allocated to interest year by year.

Total Cost

There's a difference between the total amount of your payments and your total cost. The total cost is what's allotted to *interest.*

According to the standard method of amortizing loans, part of each payment goes for interest and part goes to pay off the principal—the original amount of the loan.

Table 4.1 shows how the amortization process works for a

9 percent loan. The amount allotted to interest gradually decreases over the life of the loan, and the amount allotted to the principal gradually increases. At any particular time, your equity in your house is the market value minus the remaining loan balance. That's what you own.

You should be aware that the amortization schedule varies with the interest rate. In table 4.1, about 93 percent of the first year's payments are allotted to interest. If you have a mortgage with a lower interest rate, a smaller percentage will be allotted to interest in the first year. Similarly, a mortgage with a higher rate will have a higher percentage devoted to interest in the early years. But this should not affect your decision about which mortgage to accept.

Closing Costs

These are advance charges. They include *points* (a point is 1 percent of the loan amount) and several other kinds of charges.

There are two kinds of points. *Origination points* are the bank's standard up-front fee of usually two or three points. *Discount points* are optional. If you choose to pay an extra point or so, the bank will give you a lower interest rate.

Closing costs vary widely from one part of the country to another. They usually add up to several thousand dollars. Worksheet 4.1 shows how to add up the closing costs for different kinds of loans.

The Effective Interest Rate

When you're shopping for a mortgage, you'll probably find that you're offered different combinations of interest rates and points. For example, you may be offered a choice between a 9 percent mortgage with three points up front and a 9.25 percent mortgage with two points. How can you determine which is better?

What you have to figure out is your *effective* interest rate. That will depend on three things: the contract interest rate, the number of points, and the length of time you plan to live in

WORKSHEET 4.1 **HOW TO ESTIMATE CLOSING COSTS**

1. Origination points $_____
2. Discount points   _____
3. Application fee   _____
4. Credit check   _____
5. Your lawyer's fee   _____
6. Bank lawyer's fee   _____
7. Title search   _____
8. Title insurance   _____
9. Appraisal   _____
10. Inspections   _____
11. Local taxes and transfer fees   _____
12. Other fees   _____
13. Prepayment fee, if any   _____
14. Calculate 10% for miscellaneous   _____
     costs
15. Total closing costs $_____

If you're refinancing, add the following:

16. Present monthly payment   _____
17. Minus new monthly payment   _____
18. Difference $_____
19. Divide line 15 by line 18   _____ months

Line 19 shows how long it will take to work off the up-front costs. If you're planning to keep your house at least that many months, it will pay to refinance.

SOURCE: HSH Associates, Butler, N.J.

your new home. Table 4.2 shows how to figure the effective rate. In this example, which assumes that the borrower will live in the house for 10 years, the 9 percent mortgage with three points turns out to be the better deal. That is, it has a lower effective interest rate.

The longer you live in your house, the less important the

TABLE 4.1 HOW A LOAN IS AMORTIZED

Example: 30-year loan for $100,000 at 9 percent interest. $804.62 monthly payment, or $9,655.44 per year.

(Figures are rounded to the nearest dollar.)

YEAR	INTEREST PAID	INTEREST AS PERCENTAGE OF ANNUAL PAYMENT	PRINCIPAL PAID	PRINCIPAL AS PERCENTAGE OF ANNUAL PAYMENT	REMAINING LOAN BALANCE
1	$8,973	92.9	$682	7.1	$99,317
2	8,908	92.3	747	7.7	98,570
3	8,837	91.5	818	8.5	97,752
4	8,761	90.7	894	9.3	96,858
5	8,677	89.9	978	10.1	95,880
6	8,585	88.9	1,070	11.1	94,810
7	8,485	87.9	1,170	12.1	93,640
8	8,356	86.5	1,299	13.5	92,341
9	8,255	85.5	1,400	14.5	90,941
10	8,124	84.1	1,531	15.9	89,410
11	7,980	82.7	1,675	17.3	87,735
12	7,823	81.0	1,832	19.0	85,903
13	7,651	79.2	2,004	20.8	83,899
14	7,463	77.3	2,192	22.7	81,707
15	7,258	75.2	2,397	24.8	79,310
16	7,033	72.8	2,622	27.2	76,688

Year	Interest	%	Principal	%	Loan Balance
17	6,787	70.3	2,868	29.7	73,820
18	6,518	67.5	3,137	32.5	70,683
19	6,224	64.5	3,431	35.5	67,252
20	5,902	61.1	3,753	38.9	63,499
21	5,550	57.5	4,105	42.5	59,394
22	5,165	53.5	4,490	46.5	54,904
23	4,744	49.1	4,911	50.9	49,993
24	4,283	44.4	5,372	55.6	44,621
25	3,778	39.1	5,877	60.9	38,744
26	3,227	33.4	6,428	66.6	32,316
27	2,624	27.2	7,031	72.8	25,285
28	1,965	20.4	7,690	79.6	17,595
29	1,244	12.9	8,411	87.1	9,184
30	471	4.9	9,184	95.1	0
	$189,651		$100,000		

This table shows how the amount allocated to interest can change over the life of a mortgage loan. At first, nearly all of the annual payment is considered interest, which is deductible from your income tax. But the amount allocated to interest gradually decreases from year to year. In any particular year, your equity (your share of ownership in the property) is the current market value minus the remaining loan balance.

TABLE 4.2   FIGURING THE BEST MIX OF INTEREST RATES AND
             POINTS

Example A: 9 percent mortgage with three points
Example B: 9.25 percent mortgage with two points

	EXAMPLE A	EXAMPLE B	YOUR OPTION A	YOUR OPTION B
Mortgage interest rate	9.00%	9.25%	____	____
Multiplied by number of years you plan to be in the home	10	10	____	____
Equals	90.00%	92.50%	____	____
Plus mortgage points	3.00%	2.00%	____	____
Equals	93.00%	94.50%	____	____
Divided by number of years you plan to be in the home	10	10	____	____
Equals effective interest rate	9.30%	9.45%	____	____

When you're shopping for a mortgage, you'll probably have
a choice of different combinations of interest rates and
points. You can select the best combination by calculating
your effective interest rate, which includes any interest
costs paid in advance. Your effective rate will depend on
three factors: the contract interest rate, the number of
points, and the length of time you plan to stay in your
home. Generally, the longer you plan to keep your home,
the less points will matter. But if you plan to keep your
home only a few years, be sure to calculate the effective
rates for any mortgages you consider.

---

points become. If you amortize three points over 30 years, the
cost per year would hardly matter. But if you have to amortize
three points over, say, three years, your effective rate will be
significantly higher than your contract rate.

So, if you're not planning to live in the house very long, and you have a choice of various combinations of interest rates and points, be sure to go through the calculations above. The lower the effective rate, the better.

Income Requirements

Naturally, a bank won't give you a loan if you can't afford one. They may measure your eligibility several ways, all of them dictated by Fannie Mae. They'll certainly consider the 28/36 ratio.

The 28 Part: The bank will want to calculate what your loan payments, property taxes, and premiums for homeowner's insurance will total in the course of a year. And they'll want to know how that compares with your total family income (wages, investment income, other business income). If the housing costs are more than 28 percent of your total income, the bank may not give you a loan.

The 36 Part: The bank will also want to know what your total debt obligations are. They'll want to know the total amount that you'll need to pay for your mortgage loan, automobile loan, personal loan, credit card balances, and other obligations such as alimony. If the total comes to more than 36 percent of total income, that may be grounds for rejection.

The bank will probably have other requirements too, such as a steady employment history and a good credit record. If you think you're going to have trouble meeting those requirements, it may be appropriate to apply for a 30-year loan instead of a shorter-term loan. That way, your monthly payments will be lower and you'll have a better chance of having your loan application approved.

The rules are different for loans insured by the Federal Housing Administration (FHA) and the Veterans Administration (VA). The housing-cost and total-debt limits are more liberal, and there are some fairly tight limits on how much you can borrow. Of course, you have to be a U.S. veteran to qualify for a VA loan.

TABLE 4.3   HOW MUCH HOUSE CAN YOU AFFORD?

GROSS INCOME	MAXIMUM PRICE	DOWN PAYMENT	MORTGAGE AMOUNT
$ 30,000	$ 97,000	$19,000	$ 78,000
40,000	129,000	26,000	103,000
50,000	161,000	32,000	129,000
60,000	194,000	39,000	155,000
70,000	226,000	45,000	181,000
80,000	259,000	52,000	207,000
90,000	291,000	58,000	233,000
100,000	324,000	65,000	259,000

Assumptions: 30-year mortgage, 20 percent down payment, with mortgage payment equal to 25 percent of family income. (This allows an additional 3 percent of income for real estate taxes and homeowner's insurance, which may not be enough in all regions of the United States.) Figures are based on a mortgage rate of 9 percent. For higher incomes, simply multiply the amounts in the table.

SOURCE: *Consumer Reports,* January 1992

Collateral

In the case of a mortgage loan, you agree to put up your house as collateral. If you default on the loan, the bank can sell your home to pay the balance of the loan. You receive what's left.

Having a fairly solid piece of collateral reduces the bank's risk in taking on the loan. Consequently, the interest rates for mortgage loans are relatively low.

But you should be aware of your ownership rights. When your car is collateral for a car loan, the bank owns the car until you pay off the loan. If you default, the bank repossesses the car. With a mortgage, you continue to own the house. If you default, the bank has to take you to court to stake its claim. The bank then must request foreclosure to take over the property. This is one reason why mortgage loans are so much more complicated than other kinds of loans.

Down Payment

Most lenders require that you make a down payment of between 10 and 20 percent of the purchase price. The idea is to make sure the borrower has a good reason to live up to the loan agreement. A borrower who pays nothing down has nothing to lose.

If you pay less than 20 percent down, the bank may require that you take out mortgage insurance. If you default, the insurance company will reimburse the bank.

Prepayment Penalty

Sometimes banks impose a penalty if you pay off the loan ahead of time. Make sure that your loan agreement has no such provision.

Tax-deductibility

One of the main incentives in buying a house is that you can deduct your interest payments from your taxable income. As Table 4.1 shows, in the first few years nearly all of the amount you pay the bank is considered interest. In fact, for the first 22 years, the amount paid in interest exceeds the amount paid to reduce the principal.

The points you pay in advance are considered part of your interest payment and are therefore deductible. Other advance fees are not. If you pay $3,000 in points, you can deduct that amount from your taxable income for that year.

The rules may be different if you're refinancing. The points are still deductible, but you may not be able to deduct the entire amount the first year. You may have to deduct this charge in installments, over the life of the loan. It depends on whether the loan is completely new or a revision of the original loan.

Inflation Effects

Inflation has averaged about 4 percent a year for the last decade. If we assume that this trend will continue, how will it affect the total cost of your loan?

Your loan will be paid off in dollars that decrease in value every year. There's no point in showing the arithmetic, since the inflation rate will vary from year to year. However, you should understand that your total interest cost will be substantially reduced by even fairly low rates of inflation.

Reviewing the Effects of Taxes and Inflation

Table 4.4 shows the total costs in the mortgage example we've discussed in this chapter. In the table, we start out with a nominal cost of $192,651 and end up with a real after-tax cost of $116,766. In other words, the tax breaks and the effect of inflation reduce the cost by about 40 percent. For someone in the highest tax bracket, the cost would be reduced by almost 50 percent.

TABLE 4.4   HOW TO FIGURE REAL MORTGAGE COSTS

Example: 30-year loan for $100,000 at 9 percent interest

Total paid to bank (including three points)	$292,651
Minus the principal	100,000
Equals nominal cost	$192,651
Minus tax deductions*	63,575
Equals nominal after-tax cost	$129,076
Minus inflation effect†	12,310
Real after-tax cost	$116,766

*33% marginal tax rate
†4% per year

One of the advantages of investing in a home is that the interest costs are deductible from your taxable income. If you take out a 30-year loan for $100,000, you can expect to pay about twice that amount in interest over the life of the loan. But that cost can be substantially reduced in the form of *tax saving*—the amount of tax you avoid because interest is deductible. The cost is also reduced by inflation: You pay the loan off with dollars that are worth less and less each year. In this example, the real cost of the loan is only about 60 percent of the nominal cost.

You certainly don't have to go through these calculations when you're shopping for a loan. It's enough to know that the tax laws and inflation will lighten the load substantially.

ADJUSTABLE-RATE MORTGAGES

Mortgage rates, like all other interest rates, are linked directly or indirectly to the rates for Treasury securities. When Treasury rates change, or when bankers *think* Treasury rates are going to change, they adjust their rates accordingly.

As noted earlier, banks make their money by borrowing (from depositors) at one interest rate and lending at a higher rate. When interest rates are stable, it's easy for banks to maintain a profitable gap. But when the interest rates rise, the gap may disappear. And when interest rates rise *fast,* banks may end up paying their depositors higher rates than their borrowers are paying.

That's what happened in the late 1970s. Banks were forced to pay depositors higher and higher rates, but they were stuck with long-term loans (like mortgages) that brought in relatively low rates of interest. When interest rates reached record highs in 1981, many banks and savings-and-loan associations were on the edge of bankruptcy.

Bankers and other lenders realized that they had to set their mortgage rates extremely high—high enough to cover their present borrowing costs and high enough to avoid another 1970s-style squeeze in the future. They also realized that they had a promising alternative, the adjustable-rate mortgage (ARM).

ARMs were promising because they had been widely accepted in most industrialized countries for years. Some U.S. banks had been experimenting with ARMs since the mid-1970s, but they never really caught on. In view of the American consumer's long experience with conventional mortgages, it was obviously going to be tough to sell ARMs.

The conventional fixed-rate, long-term mortgage was established by the Federal Housing Administration (FHA) in the

1930s. Consumers have always liked them because they provide a sense of security. You know exactly what you have to pay every year, and you can stretch the loan out for 30 years or more.

With an ARM, you can't be sure what your payments will be next year, or any year after that. Still, you can stretch the loan out for 30 years. ARM rates are recalculated periodically (usually once a year). ARM rates are tied to a published index, usually a calculation of rates for various one-year U.S. Treasury securities, which fluctuates from year to year.

For banks, the main attraction of an ARM is to reduce the risk of tying up a loan at a fixed rate for many years. With an ARM, if Treasury interest rates rise, the borrower's monthly payments rise accordingly. When rates fall, the borrower's payments will fall as well. To persuade borrowers to accept this uncertainty, the bank offers a couple of incentives.

So far, most borrowers haven't been willing to accept the uncertainty of an ARM. Since it's possible that their monthly payments might rise substantially, most borrowers prefer to have a mortgage whose payments are the same each year.

But the incentives for accepting an ARM are worth considering. First of all, the introductory rate is usually well below the current rate for a conventional mortgage, which means you may be able to save a few thousand dollars in the first year. In addition, ARMs are constructed so that, unless something extraordinary happens to the economy, the borrower's interest costs may be lower than they would be with a conventional mortgage over the long run.

ARMs have been offered since 1984, and regardless of the incentives, consumers have generally ignored them. Banks haven't bothered to promote ARMs very heavily either, because borrowers seem to be comfortable paying the higher rates for conventional mortgages. At one point in the 1980s, when the spread between fixed rates and adjustable rates was wide, about 60 percent of new mortgages were ARMs. Since then, the proportion of ARMs has declined sharply. This is probably because the rates for conventional mortgages are much lower than they used to be, and borrowers do not feel the need to consider the alternative.

HOW AN ARM WORKS

When you're considering an ARM, there's a whole new set of factors to consider. Let's start with the index, which will vary from year to year and which will be the base for the interest rate for every year except the first.

The Index

Banks use several different indexes for setting ARM rates, but the current rate for one-year Treasury securities is by far the most common. If that index is 6 percent, that's the base for your interest rate until the next adjustment.

Since indexes vary, be sure to compare the index for different loans that are available. Generally, the lower the better, but banks may make up for a low index with a high margin. So you have to consider both the index and the margin.

The Introductory Rate

As noted above, the starting rate for an ARM is usually well below the prevailing rate for conventional mortgages. But this doesn't indicate what your rates will be in the future.

Chart 4.1 compares actual rates for conventional mortgages and introductory rates for ARMs since 1984, when today's ARMs first appeared. It shows that first-year ARM rates are usually two points or more below the comparable fixed rate.

The rates shown in Chart 4.1 reflect the current yields for Treasury securities. The rates for conventional mortgages are linked to long-term Treasury rates, as represented by, for example, the yields for 30-year bonds. The rates for ARMs are linked to short-term Treasury rates, as represented by, for example, the yields for three-month Treasury bills. Generally, short-term Treasury rates are lower than long-term rates. By the end of 1992, short-term rates reached their lowest level

CHART 4.1   FIRST-YEAR MORTGAGE RATES: FIXED-RATE
MORTGAGES VERSUS ADJUSTABLE-RATE MORTGAGES (30 YEARS)

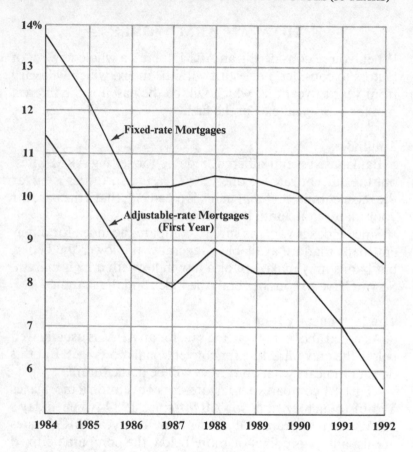

The introductory rate for ARMs is usually below the current rate for fixed-rate mortgages. Since 1984, the difference between the average rates for the two types of mortgages has been about two points. Note that interest rates on ARMs often increase substantially after the first year.

Source: HSH Associates, Butler, N.J.

since the early 1960s, while long-term rates remained fairly high.

Say you have a choice between two 30-year, $100,000 mortgages. One is a conventional mortgage at 9 percent and the other an ARM with an introductory rate of 7 percent. The first-year payments for the conventional mortgage would come to $9,655.44; for the ARM, they would come to $7,983.60. In other words, you would save $1,671.84 with the ARM.

The lower the introductory rate, the better. But don't compromise on other factors to get a low introductory rate.

The Adjustment Period

The loan agreement will specify how often the interest rate will be adjusted. A one-year period is by far the most common, and in all of the following examples we'll use this as the standard. However, you may be offered a choice of longer or shorter periods.

Caution: Some ARMs have adjustment periods shorter than a year. But for some technical reasons that we can ignore here, it's a good idea to avoid these ARMs.

The Variable Rate

After the introductory period, the rate will be adjusted periodically—for example, once a year on the anniversary of the loan. The new rate will depend on three factors—the index, the margin, and the rate caps.

The Margin

This is set for the life of the loan. A typical margin is about 2.75 percentage points. (Banks usually round off margins and rates to the nearest eighth of a point, which is .0125.)

Whenever the bank adjusts your interest rate, the new rate will be equal to the index plus the margin. If your index is 6 and your margin is 2.75, your new rate will be 8.75 percent. The margin is sometimes expressed in terms of basis points. One point of interest is equal to 100 basis points. In this case, the margin would be 275 basis points.

Chart 4.2 compares actual one-year Treasury indexes with actual rates for conventional mortgages. This index has averaged about three points below the conventional mortgage rate. The chart shows how important it is to look for a relatively low margin when you're considering an ARM. The margin will fill most of the gap between the index and the rates for conventional mortgages. The smaller the margin, the better the chance that your fully margined rate (index plus margin) will be lower than the current rates for conventional mortgages.

The average margin has gradually increased over the years, from about 2.5 in 1984 to about 2.75 recently. But when you're shopping, you may find that local lenders' ARM margins vary. Of course, there's no way to predict what the gap will be in the future. But as a general rule, you should avoid mortgages that have margins of three points or higher.

Caps and Floors

Although the basic interest rate will be tied to the index and the margin, the loan agreement will usually specify limits on how much the rate can rise at any particular adjustment point. These limits are known as *caps*. Many loan agreements also specify rate *floors*—limits on how many points the rate can drop in a particular period.

Caps are *very* important. The usual caps for one-year ARMs are two points a year and six points for the life of the loan. Never accept a loan with rate caps that are higher than these.

Caution: Sometimes the cap doesn't apply to the first adjustment. You could start out with an unusually low introductory rate and then be hit with a large rate increase when it's time to adjust. You can avoid this kind of surprise by making sure that the cap applies to *all* adjustments.

Payment Limits

Some loan agreements include limits on how much your monthly payment can rise. For example, if your monthly payment is currently $800 and the payment limit is $500, your

CHART 4.2   ONE-YEAR TREASURY INDEXES VERSUS
FIXED-RATE MORTGAGES (30 YEARS)

The most common index for ARMs is the index for one-year Treasury securities. Since 1984, that index has averaged about three points lower than the
current rate for conventional mortgages. Note, however, that the index is
only part of the equation in determining ARM rates. Lenders tack a "margin," often of two or more percentage points, onto the index to determine
the interest rate borrowers must pay.

SOURCE: HSH Associates, Butler, N.J.

payment can rise only to $1,300 (and no higher) in the next period.

The Term

As with a conventional mortgage, you may have a choice of terms. If you choose a 15-year term instead of a 30-year term, your monthly payments will be higher but you'll pay off the loan faster, and your total cost will be lower.

Monthly Payments

Your monthly payments will change every time the interest rate is adjusted. They will depend on the new rate and the remaining balance of the loan.

Don't try to use standard amortization tables to calculate your ARM payments after the first year. They won't help, because the tables are divided into convenient periods such as 25 years or 30 years. Also, they refer to loans grouped in convenient amounts such as $100,000 or $150,000. If you acquire a 30-year ARM for $100,000 and a starting rate of 7 percent, the loan balance at the end of the first year will be $98,984.09, to be paid back in the remaining 29 years. A standard amortization table will be useless for calculating the monthly payments.

Because the calculations are complicated, there are many opportunities for error when the bank recalculates what your new payments will be. Some experts say that between 20 and 30 percent of the adjustments are wrong, either in your favor or the bank's. So it's worthwhile to ask the bank for an explanation of how it arrived at the new figures.

Closing Costs

As with conventional mortgages, you'll have to pay several charges in advance. (See Worksheet 4.1.)

Prepayment Penalty

You'll probably be able to pay off the loan ahead of time without penalty, but make sure that's specified in your contract.

THE TRACK RECORD: ARMs VERSUS CONVENTIONAL MORTGAGES

TABLE 4.5   COST COMPARISON OF TWO MORTGAGES ORIGINATED IN 1987: FIXED RATE VERSUS ADJUSTABLE RATE

Both mortgages are for $100,000 loans with 30-year terms. The margin for the ARM is 2.68 (the 1987 average); caps and floors are two points per year.

	FIXED-RATE MORTGAGE		ADJUSTABLE-RATE MORTGAGE	
	RATE	INTEREST	RATE	INTEREST
1987	10.29%	$10,266	7.95%	$ 7,920
1988	10.29	10,209	9.49	9,381
1989	10.29	10,147	11.22	10,982
1990	10.29	10,078	10.56	10,273
1991	10.29	10,001	8.56	8,256
1992	10.29	9,916	6.58	6,261
Average	10.29		9.06	
Total		60,615		53,073

Amount saved with ARM: 7,542

Percent saved with ARM: 12

The 1987 rates are from Chart 4.1. The indexes for subsequent ARM rates are from Chart 4.2. The ARM rates varied a great deal, from 6.58 to 11.29. They would have varied even more if it weren't for the two-point annual cap imposed in 1988 and the two-point annual floor imposed in 1992. The net result is that the ARM cost was $7,542 below the cost of the conventional mortgage, a saving of 12 percent. Of course, there's no guarantee that this pattern will continue.

Table 4.5 is based on figures in Charts 4.1 and 4.2. It compares two mortgages originated in 1987—a conventional mortgage and an ARM. In each case, the interest rate is the actual average for that year. It is assumed that both mortgages are for $100,000 with 30-year terms. It is also assumed that the ARM has a 2.68 margin (the average for that year) and the customary caps and floors of two percentage points a year.

If a borrower had chosen the conventional mortgage, the total interest cost for the six-year period ending in 1992 would have come to $60,615. If a borrower had chosen the ARM, the interest cost would have come to $53,073, which would be a saving of $7,542, or 12 percent.

The table shows that ARM rates can fluctuate a great deal—from 6.58 percent to 11.2 percent in this example. But what matters is how the rates average out. The average ARM rate was about a point below the comparable rate for the conventional mortgage.

Table 4.6 displays the results of calculations similar to those described in Table 4.5. It compares ARMs and conventional mortgages originated in each of the years from 1987 through 1992. In each case, it's assumed that the mortgage was still in effect at the end of 1992.

In that six-year period, the average ARM proved to be less expensive than the average conventional mortgage every year. The saving ranged from 12 percent to 34 percent.

The largest percentage saving occurred in the most recent years. One reason is that the effect of the introductory discount is strongest in the early years of an ARM. Another reason is that the gap between short-term Treasury rates (which determine ARM rates) and long-term Treasury rates (which determine the rates for conventional mortgages) has been unusually large in the early 1990s.

There is, of course, no guarantee that ARMs will continue to have this advantage. But the table does indicate that it is possible for ARM borrowers to save a substantial amount of money if they are willing to put up with the uncertainty.

ARMs VERSUS CONVENTIONAL MORTGAGES IN THE 1990s

The average ARM proved to be less expensive than the average conventional mortgage in the last few years. Should borrowers seriously consider ARMs in the future?

TABLE 4.6   MORTGAGE COST COMPARISON: 1987–92

All mortgages are for $100,000 loans with 30-year terms. The ARM margins vary (from 2.68 to 2.77), and so do the Treasury indexes (from 3.90 to 8.54). The ARM margins and floors are 2 points per year.

ASSUME MORTGAGE BEGAN JAN. 1 OF THIS YEAR:	FIXED-RATE MORTGAGE		ADJUSTABLE-RATE MORTGAGE		AMOUNT SAVED WITH ARM	PERCENT SAVED WITH ARM
	AVERAGE RATE	TOTAL COST	AVERAGE RATE	TOTAL COST		
1987	10.29%	$60,615	9.06%	$53,073	$7,542	12%
1988	10.46	51,563	9.13	44,919	6,644	13
1989	10.44	41,307	8.57	33,785	7,522	18
1990	10.19	30,319	7.87	23,318	7,001	23
1991	9.40	18,685	6.86	12,612	6,073	33
1992	8.50	8,471	5.61	5,576	2,895	34

This table is based on calculations similar to those in Table 4.5. The table reflects the annual averages of four factors: the current rate for fixed-rate mortgages, the current rate for ARMs, the current one-year Treasury index, and the current margin for ARMs. The table assumes that the mortgages began on January 1 of the year indicated and were still in effect at the end of 1992.

In the six-year period, the average ARM proved less expensive than the average fixed-rate mortgage originated in the same year. The saving ranged from 12 percent to 34 percent. The largest percentage saving occurred in the most recent years for two reasons. First, the effect of the first-year discount is strongest in the early years of an ARM. Second, the gap between short-term Treasury rates (which determine ARM rates) and long-term Treasury rates (which determine the rates for conventional mortgages) has been unusually large recently.

Of course, it's impossible to predict how long ARM rates will continue to be lower than rates for conventional mortgages.

First of all, ARMs aren't for everyone. You have to have the right temperament. You have to be able to accept a certain amount of risk—the possibility that interest rates might rise and your borrowing costs could go higher than they would with a conventional mortgage. If you can't or don't want to live with this uncertainty, you'll be better off with a conventional mortgage.

An ARM with the usual caps (two points per year, six for the life of the loan) will prove risky only if the interest rate reaches its six-point maximum in three years *and* the index continues to rise. And even within that possibility, there's no risk until the fourth or fifth year of the loan.

Chart 4.3 explains why. Three different mortgages are compared in this example. All three are $100,000, 30-year loans. One is a conventional mortgage at 9 percent; the other two are ARMs with introductory rates of 6 and 7 percent. (A spread of two or three points between ARM rates and conventional rates has been common in the early 1990s.) Both ARMs have standard caps.

In this case—the worst possible case for ARMs—it's assumed that the ARM rates rise two points in each of the first three adjustment periods. That means the rates reach their lifetime limit in the fourth year, when one ARM is at 12 percent and the other is at 13 percent. It's also assumed that the indexes for these loans continue to rise.

Notice that the ARM with the higher rate is cheaper than the conventional mortgage until the fourth year. The ARM with the lower rate is cheaper than the conventional mortgage until the fifth year.

In any case, ARM rates will continue to fluctuate along with short-term Treasury rates. For the ARM borrower, what matters is not the highs and lows but how the rates average out.

The Convertible ARM

If you're interested in an ARM but skeptical about the eventual cost, one answer may be a *convertible* ARM. This is a stan-

CHART 4.3   HOW RISKY ARE ADJUSTABLE-RATE MORTGAGES?

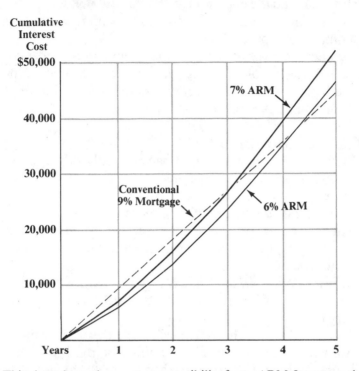

This chart shows the worst-case possibility for an ARM. It assumes that the interest rate increases to the 6-point maximum in the first three adjustments and stays at that level.

The chart compares three 30-year, $100,000 mortgages: an ARM with a first-year rate of 6 percent, an ARM with a first-year rate of 7 percent, and a conventional mortgage with a rate of 9 percent. It assumes that at the end of the third year, the ARMs reach their lifetime maximums of 12 and 13 percent, respectively. At that point, the cumulative cost of the ARM that started out at 7 percent will begin to exceed the cumulative cost of the conventional mortgage. At the end of the fourth year, the cumulative cost of the ARM that started out at 6 percent will begin to exceed the cumulative cost of the conventional mortgage.

However, under normal circumstances, the indexes for ARMs can be expected to fluctuate. In other words, there's no reason to believe that an ARM rate would remain at a permanently high plateau.

dard one-year ARM with the option of converting to a fixed-rate mortgage. You can convert at any time between the end of the first year and the end of the fifth year. But if you convert, you'll have to pay the current fixed rate plus a premium of perhaps a quarter of a percentage point.

Some lenders charge nothing for the option, and others may add another quarter of a point to your basic rate. If you convert, you'll have to pay a fee that may come to a few hundred dollars. But that's cheaper than refinancing.

Guidelines for Selecting an ARM

It's important to select the right package. All of the following key factors have to be considered:

1. *The interest-rate trend.* Never choose an ARM during an extended period of rising interest rates, or when the index has risen rapidly in the two preceding years—say two points a year.

2. *Adjustment period and index.* Pick an ARM with a one-year adjustment period and a standard one-year Treasury index.

3. *Caps.* Make sure the ARM will have the usual caps—two points per year and six points for the life of the loan—and that the cap applies to the first year.

4. *Introductory rate.* The lower the first-year rate, the better.

5. *The margin.* Be sure to check with several different lenders to find out what the typical margins are. Avoid a mortgage that has an unusually high margin, because you'll be stuck with it for the life of the loan.

6. *Second-year costs.* You can get some idea of what your second-year costs will be by adding the current index and the margin. That gives you the fully margined rate. Ideally, it should be a point or so below the current rates for a new conventional mortgage.

7. *Prepayment.* Make sure that you'll be able to pay the mortgage off ahead of time without penalty.

Shopping for Mortgages

Worksheet 4.2 shows how to collect the essential information from several lenders. If you collect ARM data, don't limit your analysis to the first year. After all, your interest rate is sure to be higher the second year. You won't be able to predict exactly what the second-year rate will be, because the index may change. But if you assume that the index won't change significantly, at least you can get some idea of what your second-year payments will be.

Homebuyer's Mortgage Kit (HSH Associates, $20) contains a helpful booklet and worksheets, a printout of data on mortgages offered by lenders in your area, and a way to get additional information on up to four mortgages that are of interest to you. To order this kit, call HSH Associates at 800-873-2387.

REFINANCING YOUR MORTGAGE

When mortgage rates reached new lows in the early 1990s, many people with conventional mortgages rushed to refinance at a lower rate. Was this a good move? How can you tell when it makes sense to refinance?

It depends on three factors: (1) how much you'll save on your monthly payments, (2) how much the refinancing charges are, and (3) how long you plan to keep your house.

Table 4.7 shows two examples of a 30-year conventional $100,000 loan at 10 percent, which is replaced by a similar loan at 8 percent. In one case, the refinancing cost comes to $3,000; in the other, it comes to $5,000. It will take about 21 months to work off the lower cost and 35 months to work off the higher cost. Under these circumstances, refinancing would pay if you planned to stay in your house for at least as long as it takes to work off the loan costs.

Does it ever make sense to refinance an ARM? You would have to consider the same three factors. But because an ARM is, in effect, a continually refinancing loan (without the refinancing costs), it would be hard to find a new ARM with a

WORKSHEET 4.2   **CHECKLIST FOR MORTGAGE SHOPPING**

Name of lender	_____
Type of loan	□ Fixed rate □ ARM
Loan amount	$_____
Term of loan	_____ years
Points (converted to dollars)	$_____
Contract interest rate	_____%
Annual percentage rate (APR)	_____%
First-year payments	$_____

For ARM calculations:

Type of index	□ One-year Treasury □ Other: _____
Present level of index	_____ points
Margin	_____ points
Annual cap	_____ points
Lifetime cap	_____ points
Second-year payments (assume index doesn't change)	$_____

Questions to ask:

Prepayment penalty?	□ Yes □ No
Does ARM cap apply to first year?	□ Yes □ No

rate low enough to justify the cost of going through all of the refinancing paperwork.

In any event, if you're thinking of refinancing, make a careful calculation of the costs of switching. Again, Worksheet 4.1 will help.

TABLE 4.7   WHEN DOES IT PAY TO REFINANCE?

Example: 30-year, $100,000, fixed-rate mortgage. Old rate: 10 percent. New rate: 8 percent. Comparing two finance costs: $3,000 and $5,000.

Monthly payment for 10 percent mortgage	$877.57
Monthly payment for 8 percent mortgage	733.76
Saving	143.81
Months to work off $3,000 finance cost ($3,000 divided by $143.81)	21
Months to work off $5,000 finance cost ($5,000 divided by $143.81)	35

General rule: It pays to refinance if you're going to live in your house at least as long as it takes to work off the finance cost.

Refinancing makes sense if your monthly mortgage costs can be reduced enough to offset the refinancing costs. You have to compare your present monthly payments with the estimated monthly payments for a replacement mortgage. Presumably your new payments would be lower. The question is, Are they low enough? That depends on how long you plan to stay in your present house. This table shows how to make the necessary calculations.

HOME EQUITY LOANS

A home equity loan is like a combination mortgage loan and credit card account: Your house is used as collateral, and the bank gives you a line of credit that you can draw against.

The Dangers

It may be *too* easy to withdraw cash. You might run up a large loan balance and find yourself unable to repay it. If you reserve this source for major expenditures like college tuition or unreimbursed medical expenses that may be tax-deductible, you'll be better off. And as with any real estate loan, you could lose your house if you fail to repay the loan.

Loan Limits

If your house is worth $100,000 and your mortgage balance is $40,000, your equity in the house is $60,000. You can probably arrange for a home equity loan for as much as 70 percent of that amount, maybe more.

Costs

The interest rates are relatively low—much lower than the rates for most credit cards and personal loans—and up to $100,000 of the interest is tax-deductible. You'll be charged interest on your unpaid balance. The rates are usually adjustable. Like ARM rates, they're tied to an index such as the prime rate (the rate that major banks charge for short-term loans to corporations with the highest credit ratings). But few of these loans have rate caps, and some have very high lifetime payment caps.

Be sure you know exactly what the index, the adjustment periods, and the caps will be.

Terms

You can usually select a term that runs anywhere from one year to 30 years. If you select a 30-year term, for example, you can borrow at various times over the life of the loan, and you can pay all or part of the balance at any time. But you have to pay the balance at the end of the term.

Credit Line

There may be a minimum loan amount (say, $5,000), and the maximum, as noted above, will be based on your equity at the time you arrange for the loan. It's a good idea to avoid asking for more credit than you need, because the up-front charges are based on your credit line.

Advance Charges

These include charges for an appraisal, a credit report, a title search, and other processing fees.

Withdrawing Cash

You don't have to withdraw any money until you need it. But banks sometimes set minimums for each withdrawal—for example, $1,000.

Withdrawals are easy to make: The bank will send you a check, deposit the money in your savings or checking account, or give you a book of blank checks.

SECOND MORTGAGES

These are like home equity loans in the sense that the amount of the loan will depend on the equity you have in your house. They're like conventional mortgages because the interest rate is fixed (usually) and you have to pay off the loan in equal monthly installments.

REVERSE MORTGAGES

About a third of the owner-occupied homes in this country are owned free and clear. The owners don't have mortgages. Most of these owners are retired. Many are property-rich but cash-poor.

Reverse mortgages are designed to supplement owners' incomes while they are still living in their homes.

Reverse Versus Conventional Mortgages

With a conventional mortgage, the bank owns (or at least has a claim on) part of your house until you pay off the loan. With each additional monthly payment, the proportion that's allotted to interest decreases and the proportion that's allotted to the principal increases. At the end, you own the house entirely and you owe the bank nothing.

With a reverse mortgage, you own your house at the beginning of the loan. Month by month, the bank pays you a fixed amount of money, which is part of the principal. At the same time, the bank allocates a certain amount of money as interest on the loan. The bank doesn't collect the interest month by month; it keeps track of the payments. At the end of the loan, the bank owns part of your house—an amount equal to the total recorded as interest. Then you either sell the house to pay the bank the accumulated interest, or you pay the bank with a separate fund.

The loan is terminated under any of the following conditions:

- You die (or in the case of a couple, the second spouse dies).
- You sell the house.
- You lease the house to someone else.
- You refinance.
- You don't pay your property taxes.
- You don't keep the property in good condition.

Tax Consequences

The amount paid to the borrower isn't taxable. The amount paid in interest is tax-deductible. In some cases, you can take deductions every year. In others, you can't take a deduction until all of the interest has been paid. It depends on the kind of accounting method you use. Check with a tax expert before you sign up for a reverse mortgage.

Borrowers' Qualifications

The amount you can borrow is determined by several factors: the age of the owners, the current value of the home, and the prospects for an increase in the value. Generally, the older you are, the more you can borrow, because the lender will have to make fewer payments.

Reverse mortgages are available through several private companies. The Federal Housing Administration (FHA) is authorized to insure some of these loans. It imposes some fairly strict loan limits. For example, with a home worth $100,000, a 75-year-old could borrow $47,000 and a 90-year-old could borrow $71,700.

For a list of reverse-mortgage lenders, send $1 and a stamped, self-addressed envelope to the National Center for Home Equity Conversion, 1210 East College Drive, Suite 300, Marshall, Minnesota 56258. Ask for the "Reverse Mortgage Locator."

AUTOMOBILE LOANS

The Term
Three years used to be the standard. But as the prices of cars have increased, so have the terms. Four- or five-year loans are now common. As usual, the longer-term loans have smaller monthly payments but are more expensive. Take the shortest-term loan you can afford.

Interest Rates
Since rates vary, it will pay to shop around. Be sure to check with different kinds of lenders—car dealers, banks, savings-and-loan associations, and credit unions. Some insurance companies also offer automobile loans.

The rates for used-car loans are higher than for new-car loans, and the terms are usually shorter.

Interest rates are usually fixed, but some lenders offer adjustable rates. As with adjustable-rate mortgage loans, an adjustable-rate car loan usually has a low first-year interest rate. But rate caps for automobile loans are rare, so you could run into trouble if interest rates rise significantly.

Some banks will offer a lower interest rate if you allow them to deduct your monthly payment from your savings or checking account. But then you'll probably have to keep a fairly sizable minimum balance.

Other Charges
Don't overlook the extra charges. There's usually a processing fee paid in advance, but no points. Some banks may require you to have a certain amount of insurance.

The Truth in Lending Act requires lenders to state the loan's annual percentage rate (APR), which must include the processing fee.

Tax Deductions
The interest cost on an automobile loan is not tax-deductible.

PERSONAL LOANS

It's usually less expensive to carry a personal loan than to let your credit card balance build up. Generally, the larger the loan, the lower the rates. Beyond that, rates differ widely from lender to lender, so shop around.

You may be able to reduce your cost by choosing an adjustable-rate loan. But usually there are no rate caps, so proceed with caution. If you agree to let the bank automatically deduct your payments from a savings account, you may receive a lower rate.

The lowest rates come with savings-secured loans: Your savings account is used as collateral. However, your account's interest payments are suspended until the loan is paid off. That could prove costly if you have a substantial amount of money in your account.

CREDIT CARD BALANCES

As we've noted before, if you don't pay your total credit card balance every month, or if you take a cash advance, you're borrowing money from the company that issued the card. This is a very convenient way to borrow, but it can also be quite expensive.

More than 100 million Americans have credit cards. About 25 percent of cardholders pay their balances when due and pay no interest. For those who don't pay when the bill arrives, the typical balance comes to about $2,500. These cardholders pay approximately 19 percent annually in interest, which is almost $500 in annual finance charges. These charges aren't tax-deductible.

If you're seriously interested in managing your money, you'll have to set tight limits on how far your credit card balance can rise before you take action to clear up the debt.

= 5 =

Guidelines
for Investment

For the ordinary investor in the United States, there are five
basic classes of investments—real estate, corporate stocks,
government bonds, corporate bonds, and cash (primarily in
the form of Treasury bills). Chart 5.1 shows that residential
real estate is the dominant form of investment.

The returns on these investments vary greatly, as we'll see
later on, and it's difficult to know how to choose among them.
But thanks to the efforts of independent experts, we now know
much more about financial markets than we used to.

A SCIENTIFIC VIEW
OF INVESTMENT MARKETS

In the old days, money managers relied only on their intuition
to select investments and to buy or sell at the right time. But
this approach is obsolete. It ignores a vast amount of evidence
about investment markets that has accumulated in the last 20
or 30 years. Some professors of economics and finance and
other independent researchers have made great progress in

explaining how these markets really work. Several have been awarded the Nobel prize in economics for, among other topics, their studies of investment markets.

Researchers have established a number of principles that can be useful to individual investors. Here are a few of the most important.

It's Essentially Impossible to Predict Stock Prices

Although the investment profession flourishes on the idea that superior skill in picking stocks can produce superior investment returns, evidence suggests that it's virtually impossible to determine exactly the right time to buy or sell and which stocks will perform better than others in the same class. Although prices generally trend upward, the fact that a certain stock performed well this year doesn't mean it will do well next year. It is just as likely to perform badly. The same rule applies to the stock market in general.

The Average Professional Money Manager Can't Consistently Beat the Market Averages

Since it's impossible to predict stock prices, it shouldn't be surprising that professionals as a group have a poor record of choosing stocks with superior returns. Most professional money managers aren't eager to publish the results of their efforts, so they tend to be very selective about what kinds of information they offer. But the managers of mutual funds have no choice; they're required by law to provide their performance records to the public. Although mutual fund managers are among the most competent and best-paid managers in the investment business, even they, on average, haven't been able to outperform the market.

Market Averages

The basic way to assess the performance of any portfolio of stocks is to compare it to standard market averages. The Dow Jones Industrial Average (the Dow) is the best-known market indicator. It's an average of the daily prices of stocks in 30

CHART 5.1   ASSETS OWNED BY U.S. HOUSEHOLDS

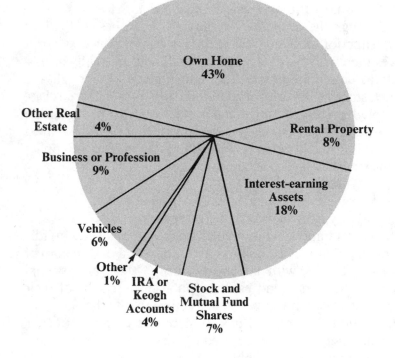

SOURCE: U.S. Bureau of the Census

leading companies in several industries—IBM, Merck, 3M, and so on. It's useful for recording day-to-day and year-to-year changes in the stock market. But since the Dow tracks the performance of only a few of the 5,000 stocks available to the public, this index is too limited to provide a comprehensive view of changes in the market.

The Standard & Poor's (S&P) 500 Stock Index is a better indicator of market changes. As the name suggests, it includes 500 leading stocks, and each stock is weighted according to its total capitalization (current price per share times the number of shares issued). The S&P represents about 70 percent of the market value of all the publicly traded U.S. stocks.

As small-company stocks have come to play such an important role in the stock market, the Wilshire 5000 has become another prominent indicator. This index records the returns of all the stocks in the S&P 500, plus 4,500 smaller-company stocks that account for most of the remaining 30 percent of the market value of all publicly traded U.S. stocks.

Mutual Funds

Table 5.1 shows that the average equity fund manager underperformed the S&P for the last 10 years. The professionals occasionally beat the S&P, but the average returns work out to 14.6 percent for the professionals and 17.6 percent for the S&P. To put this another way, the average S&P return was 20 percent higher than the average return on general equity funds.

This suggests that individual investors can beat the professionals as a group simply by investing in *index funds*. These are mutual funds that hold all of the stocks represented by a particular index (for example, the S&P 500), in proportion to their total market value. Investors in index funds have to pay a small management fee, but the average index fund should still be able to beat the average equity fund.

Pension Funds

Researchers have also studied the performance of pension funds that invest solely in corporate stocks. One recent study

TABLE 5.1   PROFESSIONAL MUTUAL FUND MANAGERS VERSUS
             THE S&P 500

(Total returns 1982–91)
Assumption: All proceeds reinvested.

	GENERAL EQUITY FUNDS	S&P 500
1982	26.03%	21.55%
1983	21.65	22.56
1984	− 1.26	6.27
1985	28.14	31.73
1986	14.37	18.67
1987	0.91	5.25
1988	15.47	16.56
1989	24.97	31.63
1990	− 6.00	− 3.11
1991	35.88	30.40
Average	14.61	17.58
(12/31/81–12/31/91)		

SOURCE: Lipper Analytical Services, Inc., New York, N.Y.

The average manager of an equity (stock) mutual fund has
underperformed the Standard & Poor's 500 index for the
last 10 years. The professionals occasionally beat the S&P,
but on average the S&P had a three-point advantage.
Under the circumstances, the individual investor may be
able to outperform the average professional over the long
run simply by investing in index funds, which are mutual
funds designed to duplicate the performance of a market
index like the S&P 500.

covered the performance of 769 pension funds in the 1983–89
period. It showed that the average fund trailed the S&P 500
index by 1.3 points. And that's *before* management fees were
subtracted. Management fees are charged because corporations assign the job of managing their pension funds to
specialists—banks, insurance companies, or investment-
counseling firms.

The authors of the study concluded that if the corporations had put the pension money into index funds or some other fund patterned on the S&P 500, corporate pension funds would be richer by $15 billion a year.

Why Do Professionals Underperform the Averages?

For one thing, the professionals have to pay brokerage commissions when they buy and sell stocks. The professionals also charge a small fee to cover their own management costs. Those costs are then subtracted from the value of the fund before the return is calculated. By contrast, the S&P 500 is nothing more than an average of the current prices of 500 stocks (weighted by the total value of each company's outstanding stock). The average doesn't reflect the costs of buying and selling any of the 500 stocks. But if the professionals can't provide returns that are high enough to offset their buying and selling costs plus their management fees, it's worth asking whether this service is necessary.

Researchers also acknowledge that professional managers may not be entirely free to run their funds as they wish. Many are employed by large institutions—pension funds, insurance companies, foundations, endowments, and mutual funds—that own half of the outstanding stock of U.S. corporations. These institutions track their fund managers' performance very carefully. Consequently, to avoid conspicuous failures, the fund managers tend to buy and sell the same stocks that their competitors are buying and selling. The most popular stocks are the stocks of prominent companies, which represent moderate risk and moderate reward. The net result is that the professional fund managers have mediocre performance records.

Since all of these professionals are basing their buying and selling decisions on the same information, which spreads very quickly through the financial community, it's extremely difficult for any one manager to outperform the competition for long. It's also logical to assume that if any of these professionals knew how to beat the market, they wouldn't share their secrets with their customers. They would spend their time guiding their own investments.

Because the professionals' performance as a group has been consistently poor, university researchers have long been skeptical about the value of professional money management. About 20 years ago, Paul Samuelson, a Nobel prize winner, said: "A respect for evidence compels me to incline toward the hypothesis that most portfolio decision makers should go out of business—take up plumbing, teach Greek, or help produce the annual GNP by serving as corporate executives." Needless to say, few if any investment managers have taken his advice.

Exceptions to the Rule

Although the average manager can't beat the market averages, there's evidence that a few managers do outperform the averages with some consistency. Later on, we'll discuss how these managers have been able to excel and how you can locate them.

The Idea of Risk Is at the Center of the Investing Process

There is no perfect investment. None is guaranteed to hold its value, and none consistently provides returns that will survive the impact of inflation and taxes. When you choose one kind of investment over another, you're essentially making a choice about risk.

Risk Is Related to Reward

Generally, the higher the risk, the higher the reward. Nothing ventured, nothing gained. This is probably the most basic idea to draw from all the research on investment management.

But you can't assume that if you make a high-risk investment, you'll necessarily be rewarded with a high return. For example, if you invest in a high-risk computer company that happens to be badly managed, you'll probably take a loss. High risk doesn't guarantee high reward.

Table 5.2 shows the annual returns for several different categories of investments over more than 60 years. These aver-

TABLE 5.2   **LONG-TERM RETURNS ON VARIOUS INVESTMENTS**
            (1926–91)

	AVERAGE TOTAL RETURN	VOLATILITY INDEX
Small-company stocks	12%	35%
Common stocks in general	10	21
Long-term corporate bonds	5	9
Intermediate-term government bonds	5	6
Long-term government bonds	5	9
U.S. Treasury bills	4	3
Inflation rates	3	5

SOURCE: © Ibbotson Associates, *Stocks, Bonds, Bills, and Inflation 1992 Yearbook* (Chicago: Ibbotson Associates). Annual updates of work originally written by Roger G. Ibbotson and Rex A. Sinquefield. Used with permission. All rights reserved.

Reward is generally related to investment risk. This table shows the average annual total return (assuming all proceeds are reinvested) for several forms of investments since 1926. It also shows a volatility index, which is a measure of risk. Corporate stocks, particularly the stocks of smaller corporations, easily outperformed government and corporate bonds.

Common stocks are those included in the S&P 500. Small-company stocks are represented by the 100 smallest companies in the S&P 500.

ages are sometimes called *expected returns* because it's reasonable to expect your average returns in the future will be fairly close to the established averages.

This table also shows a *volatility index* for each type of investment. The volatility index is based on a statistical measure called the *standard deviation,* which is one measure of risk. The higher the standard deviation, the higher the volatility and the higher the expected risk.

The returns in this table are *total* returns. They include both appreciation and income (dividends or interest). It's assumed that all income is reinvested in the original securities.

Table 5.2 shows that the inflation rate has averaged 3 percent since 1926. Remember: If you want to know your real return for any investment, you have to subtract the rate of inflation. If you have a 10 percent return and the inflation rate is 3 percent, your real return is 7 percent.

Recent research suggests that risk may be more closely related to factors other than volatility. At this point, we have to conclude that there aren't any really foolproof measures of risk. However, it's still safe to say that if you want a higher return, you'll probably have to accept more risk (or get lucky).

This is also true for professionals. A small group of mutual fund managers has compiled excellent long-term records. But in most cases these managers have either taken on extra risk or have been unusually lucky. Superior performance doesn't necessarily mean superior skill.

Select the Right *Combination* of Assets

Your portfolio is your collection of assets (stocks, bonds, real estate, whatever). Each asset has a different degree of risk.

Roger Ibbotson, the Yale economist who has studied returns on various kinds of investments for many years, says that differences in portfolio mixes account for nearly all the differences in total portfolio returns.

There's no easy way to choose the right group of assets, but it's clear that a "balanced" portfolio—one that contains securities with varying degrees of risk—will yield more satisfactory results than one that's heavily weighted toward very risky investments or toward presumably safe investments. If your new portfolio contains only low-risk or high-risk securities, you will have too many securities that are in the same phase: They will move up and down together.

If your portfolio contains only stocks, you can expect large fluctuations in portfolio value but a fairly good long-term return. On the other hand, if your portfolio contains only bonds, you can expect smaller fluctuations in portfolio value, but your returns will be lower. In either case, there's some risk because you may be forced to sell when the values are low. The best way to have a satisfactory long-term return is to have a diversified portfolio containing several types of securities.

Chart 5.2 shows how average annual returns can vary from year to year. In the period since 1970, small-company stocks have been very volatile but produced the highest average return. At the other end of the scale, Treasury bills have proved very stable but produced the lowest average return. The chart suggests that individual investors would do well to put most of their investment money into stocks but also have some money invested in more stable securities to provide a cushion in the years when stocks are performing badly.

In practice, individual investors do not live with risk. Chart 5.1 shows that the amount held in the form of interest-earning assets (mainly savings accounts, money market deposit accounts, and CDs) is nearly three times the amount held in the form of stocks and mutual funds.

LEARNING TO LIVE WITH RISK

Risk is like the bottle that some people see as half-empty and others see as half-full. Many investors see risk as the potential for loss; others see it as the potential for gain.

History is on the side of the optimists. As Table 5.2 shows, investors who chose the higher risk options and invested for the long term have beaten the inflation rate and earned a respectable return. Those investors who chose the lower risk options may have avoided losses, but they may have also avoided good gains. When you account for inflation and income taxes, there's not much left.

Individual investors' choices depend on several factors: stage of life, current income, accumulated wealth, and attitudes toward risk.

Stage of Life

If you're young and single and have opportunities to increase your income, you can afford to take on fairly substantial risk. But if you're married and have dependents, you'll have to be more cautious, especially if you're uncertain about your prospects in the job market. If you're in your sixties and have less of a chance of increasing your income, it will make sense to channel a fairly large proportion of your funds into relatively safe investments.

Current Income

If you have a fairly adequate and steady income, you can obviously take on more risk than if you have a low income.

Wealth

If you've managed to accumulate a substantial amount of wealth, you can afford to take on a lot of risk in part of your investments. If you've accumulated only a modest amount of wealth, you should be cautious about getting involved with high-risk investments.

Attitude Toward Risk

This is probably the most important factor of all. Some people are comfortable only with low-risk investments. If you're in that group, you're probably going to forgo a significant amount of return.

On the other hand, if you're capable of assuming higher risk, you may have to adjust to the possibility of occasional losses, which might be significant. Still, a temporary decline in the value of your investments isn't really a loss. You don't actually incur a loss unless you sell when the value of your investment is below what you paid for it. What matters is how your investments average out over the long run.

Most individual investors tend to *overestimate* the actual risks of various kinds of investment. They seem to respond to the possibility of risk instead of the probability of risk, as indicated by the historical record. It's likely that the more you know about the historical record, and the more you know about ways to reduce risk, the more tolerant you will be of risk.

WAYS TO REDUCE RISK

Regardless of your financial situation, your attitude toward risk, and whether you prefer high-risk or low-risk investments, you have several ways to reduce risk.

Diversification

This is essentially a matter of not putting all your eggs in one basket. The values (prices) of most investments fluctuate over the years. Fortunately, different kinds of investments reach their short-term highs and lows at different times—that is, they go through their cycles at different times. For example, domestic stocks are often out of phase with foreign stocks, and stocks are often out of phase with bonds.

Generally, the more you can spread your money over different kinds of investments, the less risky your holdings will be. But there are good and bad ways to diversify. For example, if your portfolio consists of six different growth stocks, it's not diversified. That's also true of a portfolio consisting of six different bonds.

Basically there are three levels of diversification. First, diversify across the main types of investments—stocks, bonds, cash, real estate. Then diversify within each type: Buy stocks of several companies, or buy bonds of several companies. Last, diversify geographically: Hold stocks and bonds of companies all over the globe.

Buy and Hold

As Table 5.2 indicated, annual returns on common stocks have averaged out to 10 percent over the long run. But from year to year, there have been dramatic ups and downs in stock values, as shown in Chart 5.2.

CHART 5.2   **HOW AVERAGE RETURNS VARY FROM YEAR TO YEAR (1970–91)**

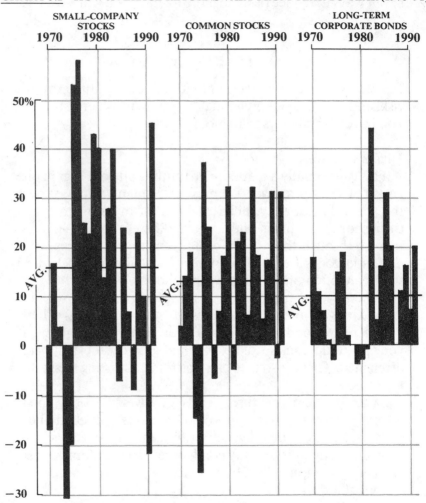

Note: Average inflation rate in 1970–92 was 6%.

This chart shows how average annual returns have varied in the last two decades. Small-company stocks have been very volatile but produced the highest average return. On the other hand, Treasury bills have been very stable with no negative returns, but the average return has been relatively low. The chart suggests that individual investors who want to take advantage of this long-term pattern should put the bulk of their investment funds

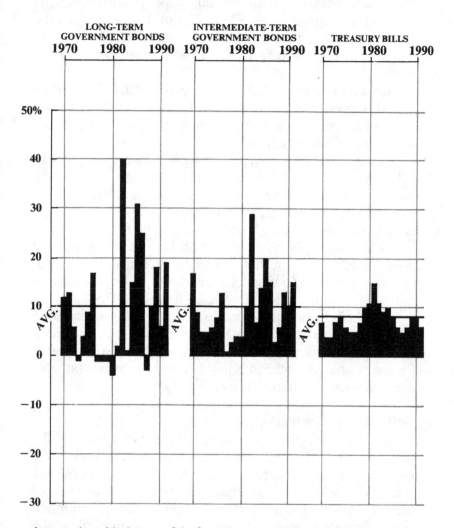

into stocks, with the rest of the funds in more stable securities to provide a cushion in the years when stocks have negative returns.

SOURCE: © Ibbotson Associates, *Stocks, Bonds, Bills, and Inflation 1992 Yearbook* (Chicago: Ibbotson Associates). Annual update of work originally written by Roger G. Ibbotson and Rex A. Sinquefield. Used with permission. All rights reserved.,

But if you buy stocks (or any other kind of security investment) and hold them for several years, you diminish the chance that you will have a loss. To put it another way, the longer you hold on to your stocks, the better the chance that you'll receive something close to the average return of 10 percent.

This is evident in Table 5.3. It shows the returns for holding periods longer than a single year—five, 10, and 20 years. As you can see, the highs and lows became closer together the longer the stocks were held.

The statistics support a buy-and-hold strategy. Buy stocks with superior returns and keep them through the ups and downs of the market. Sell only when the price is high.

Another good reason for adopting a buy-and-hold strategy is that you can avoid high transaction costs. Every time you buy or sell stock, you have to pay a broker's commission. And if you trade frequently, that will seriously reduce your return.

A buy-and-hold strategy also gives you an opportunity to put more of your money into those kinds of investments that would otherwise be considered fairly risky. The longer you're willing and able to hold on to your investments, the more emphasis you should put on stocks. By being a long-term investor in stocks, you can not only reduce your risk but also increase your potential returns.

Dollar-cost Averaging

The idea of dollar-cost averaging is to invest exactly the same amount at regular intervals (say, once every three months) year in and year out, regardless of whether the market is high or low. One advantage is that you build your investment steadily and you avoid the danger of putting too much money into the market at the wrong time and too little at the right time. (Most individual investors tend to buy when the market is rising and sell when the market is falling, which is precisely the wrong thing to do.) Another advantage is that, over the long haul, you will pay less for your shares than if you bought a fixed number of shares every time you added to your investment.

TABLE 5.3 HIGHEST AND LOWEST ANNUAL RETURNS FOR
COMMON STOCKS IN VARIOUS PERIODS, 1950-91

	HIGH	LOW	AVERAGE
One-year periods	53%	−26%	14%
Five-year periods	24	−2	12
10-year periods	19	1	11
20-year periods	13	7	9

SOURCE: © Ibbotson Associates, *Stocks, Bonds, Bills, and Inflation 1992 Yearbook* (Chicago: Ibbotson Associates). Annual update of work originally written by Roger G. Ibbotson and Rex A. Sinquefield. Used with permission. All rights reserved.

The longer you hold on to your securities, the better the chance that you will have a respectable return. This table shows how annual returns for the S&P 500 stocks have fluctuated since 1950. Although the average return was 10 percent, the highest annual return for a single year was 54 percent and the lowest was − 26 percent. In fact, in nine of those 38 years, the annual return was negative. However, if you look at the record for fairly long periods of time—five years or more—it's clear that the volatility diminishes. For example, if you take the annual returns for five-year periods, the highest average was 24 percent and the lowest was − 2 percent. That means that if you hold your stocks at least five years, you'll have a very small chance of taking a loss. If you hold your stocks for 20 years, you can probably expect to have a healthy return.

Table 5.4 shows how dollar-cost averaging works. In this case, you decide to invest $200 every three months in a particular mutual fund. In the first quarter, the price is $25 a share and you receive eight shares. In subsequent quarters, the price rises and falls. When the price is low, you receive more shares than when the price is high.

The net effect is that, at the end of 10 quarters, you've invested $2,000 and you own another 84.38 shares. The average cost is $23.70, as compared with the average price of $25. That's a 5 percent discount.

TABLE 5.4   HOW DOLLAR-COST AVERAGING WORKS

Purchase of mutual fund shares at an average price of $25

QUARTERLY PERIODS	QUARTERLY INVESTMENT	SHARE PRICES	SHARES BOUGHT
1	$200	$25	8.00
2	200	20	10.00
3	200	15	13.33
4	200	20	10.00
5	200	25	8.00
6	200	25	8.00
7	200	30	6.67
8	200	35	5.71
9	200	30	6.67
10	200	25	8.00
Total invested	$2,000		
Average share price		$25	
Shares bought			84.38

Average cost per share: $23.70

> The idea of dollar-cost averaging is to invest exactly the
> same amount at regular intervals year in and year out,
> regardless of whether the market is up or down. You'll fare
> better than if you try to time your investments to take
> advantage of ups and downs in the market. In this example,
> the investor puts $200 into a mutual fund every quarter.
> The prices of the shares in the fund fluctuate, so the inves-
> tor buys fewer shares when the price is high and more when
> the price is low. Although the price averages $25, the inves-
> tor's average cost works out to $23.70. One advantage of
> this technique is that the investor avoids the common ten-
> dency to put too much money into the market when prices
> are high and too little when prices are low.

This technique is most appropriate for buying mutual fund
shares. You invest whatever amount you want, and the shares
are divided up accordingly. If you were to buy a particular

stock through a broker, you couldn't buy partial shares and you would have to pay a broker's commission.

The catch in a dollar-averaging approach is that you have to be disciplined. You have to have the courage to invest when the market is low and everyone else is staying on the sidelines.

A dollar-cost averaging program can be used to buy shares in any kind of mutual fund.

THE HARD WAY AND
THE EASY WAY TO INVEST

Peter Lynch, the longtime manager of Fidelity's Magellan Fund and one of the most successful money managers of all time, declared his opinion of the stock market in his book *One Up on Wall Street*. He said, "Rule number one, in my book, is: Stop listening to professionals!"

But his rule number one is followed by this remark: "Twenty years in this business convinces me that any normal person using the customary three percent of the brain can pick stocks just as well as, if not better than, the average Wall Street expert." Accordingly, he devotes most of his book to explaining "how to use what you already know to make money in the market," to quote the subtitle.

It may be true that any normal person can do as well as, or better than, the average Wall Street expert. But this advice is leading the innocent into temptation. It's encouraging individuals to be do-it-yourselfers in the investment game, which can be complicated. Peter Lynch talks like a do-it-yourselfer, but his record would be almost impossible to duplicate.

Do-it-yourself investing requires either a lot of luck or a considerable amount of knowledge, time, and skill to achieve anything equal to the performance of the average professional. It also requires the discipline to trade as infrequently as possible to avoid incurring high transaction costs.

Your chances of consistently beating the market averages

are essentially zero. You, like any other stock picker, may have a good year now and then, but that's a matter of chance.

Doing it yourself is the hard way. The easy way is to buy the services of a professional. But not just *any* professional—no brokers, counselors, newsletter writers, forecasters, or any other professional who doesn't have a well-established, published record. Rule number one should be: Stop listening to professionals, except those who run index funds or mutual funds that have excellent performance records.

As noted earlier, professional fund managers build good records by taking extra risk, or by being lucky in selecting stocks that have performed better than expected. If you're not interested in extra risk, you can play it safe by investing in index funds. That's the easiest way of all.

REINVESTING YOUR PROCEEDS

It's worth repeating that the returns listed in Table 5.2 are based on the assumption that all dividend or interest income is reinvested. That's a good practice for individual investors, as long as you don't need that income to pay your living expenses. If you don't reinvest the proceeds, your long-term returns will be much lower than they could be.

An analysis by Ibbotson Associates shows that a dollar invested in common stocks at the end of 1925, with dividends reinvested, grew to $675.59 by the end of 1991. That represents a compound annual growth rate of 10.4 percent, which is rounded off to 10 percent in Table 5.2. But if the dividends were not reinvested, that dollar would have increased to only $32.70 in the same period. That represents a compound growth rate of 5.4 percent. The $32.70 is the *capital appreciation,* which is simply the increase in value of the asset regardless of any dividends it may have earned.

The best way to build your investment is to reinvest the proceeds consistently.

SELECTING A GOOD INVESTMENT MIX

Asset allocation is the current term for diversifying your assets in a systematic way. The goal is to pick the combination of assets that will provide the highest average return, in keeping with the amount of risk you're willing to accept.

As we'll see in chapter 7, it's important for you to own your own home if you possibly can. But because every home is different, it's difficult to determine real estate values at any particular time. (It's not like looking up the price in the stock pages of your daily newspaper.) And because every family's financial situation is different, it's impossible to say how much of your investment portfolio should be devoted to real estate. So we'll limit this discussion to the non–real estate part of your portfolio.

Selecting portfolio assets is a two-step process. The first and most important step is to decide how much of the portfolio should be devoted to relatively risky assets like stocks. You'll also have to decide how much should be devoted to more stable, low-risk assets like bonds and cash equivalents. Obviously, an elderly person would want to invest in the low-risk end of the spectrum. A young, single executive might want to invest in the high-risk end.

The second step is to select the assets to be included in the riskier part of the portfolio.

Table 5.5 shows how your returns are affected by what you include in your portfolio. In this case, the choice is between two assets—stocks and long-term government bonds. The differences in the five portfolios vary from 9 to 13 percent. That may not seem like much until you put it in dollar terms. An all-stock portfolio earning $1,300 a year yields half again as much as an all-bond portfolio earning $900.

When you decide what kinds of assets to have in your portfolio, be sure to include any assets you may have in company retirement plans and elsewhere. Table 5.6 shows five different ways to arrange your non–real estate assets, ranked according to risk. Keep in mind that every adviser will suggest a different

TABLE 5.5   HOW PORTFOLIO RETURNS ARE AFFECTED BY ASSET
            CHOICES

Example: Portfolios consisting of various combinations of stocks
and long-term government bonds. Calculations are based on the
average total returns from 1970 to 1991, as shown in Chart 5.2.

PERCENTAGE OF PORTFOLIO, STOCKS TO BONDS	EXPECTED ANNUAL RETURN
100–0	13%
75–25	12
50–50	11
25–75	10
0–100	9

Although it's a good idea to diversify your investments,
keep in mind that your total portfolio return will depend
on whether you lean toward high-risk or low-risk investments. This table shows how returns are affected by split-
ting funds between two types of investments—corporate
stocks and long-term government bonds. In the long run
this portfolio will have the highest expected return if it's
devoted entirely to stocks and the lowest expected return if
it's devoted entirely to bonds. But there are compromises
that may yield a reasonable return without leaning too far
in one direction or the other.

combination of investments. These examples are a starting
point for developing your plan.

Financial advisers sometimes suggest mathematical for-
mulas to help you allocate your assets, but basically it's your
decision. You are the only person who can decide how to balance your portfolio. Your decision should be based on the
degree to which you see risk as a problem or as an opportunity.

GUIDELINES

1. **Invest for the long term.** Decide how you want to allocate your investment dollars among stocks, bonds, cash,

TABLE 5.6 **FIVE DIVERSIFIED PORTFOLIOS**

(excluding real estate)

	LOW RISK	LOW-TO-MEDIUM RISK	MEDIUM RISK	MEDIUM-TO-HIGH RISK	HIGH RISK
Cash equivalents	10%	10%	10%	10%	10%
Short-term bonds	30	30	25	20	10
Intermediate-term bonds	30	25	20	10	5
Long-term bonds	10	15	10	10	10
Common stocks	20	20	25	30	35
Small-company stocks			10	20	30
	100%	100%	100%	100%	100%

Here are five different ways you might diversify your portfolio, depending on your attitude toward risk.

97

and real estate. Then stick with that decision until your economic situation changes significantly. Review your investments periodically—say, once or twice a year—but don't worry about short-term fluctuations in prices.

2. **Diversify.** Spread your money around. Put it in high-, medium-, and low-risk investments, in whatever proportions you feel comfortable with. Put some money in domestic investments and some in foreign investments.

3. **Put your money in mainstream investments.** Invest in tried-and-true instruments like stocks and bonds. Don't be tempted to invest in commodities, options, real estate partnerships, or any complicated investment products that someone may try to sell you.

4. **Invest in securities through index funds or mutual funds that have consistently delivered higher returns.** Avoid the temptation to pick individual stocks and bonds on your own: Very few people are good at that. A small number of the more than 3,000 mutual funds have consistently provided higher-than-average returns. Superior past performance doesn't guarantee superior future performance, but there's some evidence that fund managers who have performed exceptionally well in the recent past can be expected to do so in the future.

5. **Invest on a regular schedule.** Whether the market is up or down, put the same amount of money into your investments periodically—say, once a month, once every six months, or once a year.

6. **For a good long-term return, concentrate on stock funds.** Stocks are relatively risky, but if you buy and hold, then sell only when stock prices are high, you'll increase your chances of receiving a respectable return.

7. **Reinvest all of your proceeds.** That's how the real gains are made.

8. **Buy low, sell high.** Trite but right. As noted earlier, many individual investors—perhaps most of them—do the

opposite. They sell when their investments are in a slump and buy when they spot an investment that's soaring.

9. **Patience, patience.** For the individual investor, building wealth is a long, slow process: three steps forward, one step back. But for the investor who stays on track, the rewards can be substantial.

— 6 —

Mutual Funds

Mutual funds offer individual investors an easy, efficient way to channel savings into stocks, bonds, cash equivalents, real estate, and almost any other kind of investment. Mutual funds have been sold since the 1920s. The number grew very slowly for years, and by 1980 there were about 500 different funds. Then they really took off. There are now more than 3,000 funds with a total of about 60 million shareholders.

Here are some of the factors that have made mutual funds popular:

Availability of Detailed Information

Both *Business Week* and *Forbes* publish annual performance summaries for several hundred funds. *Consumer Reports* publishes summaries occasionally. These summaries typically include the following:

- *Ratings* of each fund based on annual returns and apparent risk
- *Size* of the fund in terms of assets owned

- *Fees* the managers charge for managing the fund
- *Investment objectives*—for example, whether the fund concentrates on growth or income, or on particular industries
- *Annual returns* for the most recent periods of, say, one, three, five, and ten years
- *Trends* in the fund's performance
- *Turnover* of assets. Some funds are very active traders, and some are not
- *Risk* of the fund's investments
- *Telephone number* for more information on how the fund is managed and how to become a shareholder in the fund

Convenience

If you're interested in a particular fund, call the company and ask for more details. You will receive brochures describing the fund, a prospectus (a detailed description required by law), and an application form. You can invest by sending in an application and a check for the minimum amount required. After that, you can usually handle all transactions by phone or mail.

When you invest in a mutual fund, you buy shares in the fund itself, which in turn buys stocks or other securities issued by other companies. But you don't have to buy a whole number of shares, as you would if you were buying stocks through a broker. With a mutual fund, you might send in $1,000 and become owner of 53.333 shares in the fund. The price of a share is calculated as follows: total net assets (assets minus liabilities) divided by the number of shares issued by the fund.

You'll receive periodic reports on the number and value of the fund shares you own. The values, or prices, change every day, and you can check on them in the mutual fund tables in major newspapers. Prices are stated in terms of *net asset value* (NAV), or the total value of all the securities the fund owns, minus the fund's operating costs and divided by the number of shares owned by all of the fund's shareholders.

Mutual funds are required to pay 98 percent of their earnings to shareholders every year. Most funds will arrange to have your proceeds reinvested automatically, if you wish. Some will arrange to have a fixed amount periodically transferred from your checking account for investment in new shares.

Liquidity

If you invest in a mutual fund, the fund will buy your shares back at any time, at the current price. All you have to do is call and ask for a check.

Wide Range of Choices in Types of Funds

Most funds are open-end funds. Anyone can buy in at any time, and the number of shares expands with the total amount invested. Some funds are closed-end funds. In this case, the fund issues a limited number of shares when it starts up, and the only way an investor can acquire these shares is to buy them from a broker. For the individual investor, open-end funds make the most sense.

Beyond these two basic types of funds, there are many variations. We'll discuss the differences later. You can put your money into dozens of different kinds of investments without the wear and tear of conducting research, arranging for trades, and keeping records on individual corporations' stocks and bonds for tax purposes.

Professional Management

If professional managers as a group can't consistently beat the market, why depend on the services of any professionals? The fact is that some professionals have excellent records. Those are the ones you want to hire. Carefully review published performance records, and avoid those funds that haven't done as well as other funds in the same category.

Diversification

Mutual fund managers generally invest the fund's money in many different securities. At one point, the largest stock fund, Fidelity Investments' Magellan Fund, owned stock in about

1,400 different companies. Funds that invest in stocks are often called equity funds, because stocks represent equity in, or ownership of, the companies. Most big equity funds hold stocks in 200 or more companies. This gives the fund's shareholders the advantage of diversification without the disadvantage of having to pick the stocks to be included in their portfolio.

But most funds concentrate on a specific part of the market—for example, high-growth stocks or high-income stocks. So, for the individual investor, it's appropriate to further diversify by investing in four or five different kinds of mutual funds, maybe more. An investor might select a money market mutual fund (low risk), a bond fund (moderate risk), a stock fund (higher risk), and a fund specializing in foreign securities (varying degrees of risk).

Relatively Low Operating Costs

The average stock fund subtracts about 1.5 percent of the fund's value every year to cover operating costs. If you were to manage your portfolio yourself and were in the habit of buying and selling frequently, your operating costs would probably be higher. However, there are some additional costs that vary from fund to fund. We'll discuss those later.

TYPES OF MUTUAL FUNDS

The mutual fund industry has developed a number of labels that are supposed to give investors some idea of each fund's stated objectives. The trouble is that two funds in the same category may invest in quite different kinds of securities. One fund may actually take on more risk than the other and therefore have higher returns in some years. The unwary investor may conclude that the fund with the higher return is more skillfully managed. But the fact is that a higher return usually means that the fund owns riskier securities. In any case, what you should keep in mind is that the labels are only very loose indicators of how the funds operate.

Table 6.1 lists the main types of funds ranked roughly in

TABLE 6.1   BASIC TYPES OF MUTUAL FUNDS RANKED FROM
             LOW TO HIGH RISK

TYPE	INVESTMENTS
Money market	• Government securities with maturities (lives) of less than one year • Certificates of deposit (CDs) • Commercial paper (short-term loans to corporations)
Short-term bonds	• Government and corporate bonds with maturities of one to five years
Intermediate-term bonds	• Government and corporate bonds with maturities of five to ten years
Long-term bonds	• Government and corporate bonds with maturities of 15 to 30 years
Income	• Bonds and stocks that pay high dividends
Balanced	• Bonds and stocks that pay moderate dividends and have moderate growth
Index	• Stocks that are represented in a market index, like the Standard & Poor's 500
Equity income	• Stocks that pay high dividends
Growth and income	• Stocks that pay high dividends and have good growth
High-yield bonds	• High-risk corporate bonds, including "junk" bonds
Growth	• Stocks in companies that have fast-rising earnings and/or revenues
Global equity	• Stocks of U.S. and foreign companies
International equity	• Stocks of foreign companies
Real estate	• Stocks of real estate companies

TYPE	INVESTMENTS
Sector	• Stocks of a particular industry, such as health care
Small company	• Stocks of relatively small, fast-growing companies
Aggressive growth	• Stocks of very fast-growing companies
Precious metals	• Stocks in companies that mine gold and other precious metals

For the individual investor, buying shares in mutual funds is the most convenient way to invest. There are many ways to classify mutual funds. In this table, they're ranked roughly according to risk. The wise investor will diversify mutual fund investments to include several funds with varying degrees of risk.

---

order of risk, from the lowest to the highest. Long-term bonds are near the middle of the risk spectrum. To repeat an earlier note of caution, higher-risk investments tend to have higher returns, but that's not always true. Sometimes high-risk investments turn out to have relatively low returns, and sometimes low-risk investments produce higher returns than you would normally expect.

Some of the funds listed in Table 6.1 can be classified in other ways. Here are a few important distinctions.

Taxable Versus Tax-Exempt Funds

Some funds invest in bonds and other securities issued by municipalities—states, counties, cities, and other local authorities. The advantage of these funds is that they are exempt from federal income tax. But since the returns are low, you have to do some calculations to see whether it will pay to invest in *municipals,* as they're called.

Table 6.2 shows how to compare the return on tax-exempt securities with similar securities that are subject to federal

TABLE 6.2   HOW TO COMPARE TAX-FREE RETURNS WITH
            TAXABLE RETURNS

RETURN ON TAX-FREE SECURITY	EQUIVALENT RETURN ON A TAXABLE SECURITY		
	15% MARGINAL BRACKET	28% MARGINAL BRACKET	31% MARGINAL BRACKET
5%	5.88%	6.94%	7.24%
6	7.06	8.33	8.70
7	8.24	9.72	10.14
8	9.41	11.11	11.59
9	10.59	12.50	13.04
10	11.76	13.89	14.49
11	12.94	15.28	15.94
12	14.12	16.67	17.93

Securities issued by states, counties, cities, and other local
authorities are generally exempt from federal income tax.
This may make them particularly attractive to investors in
high tax brackets. The problem is that these investments—
known as municipals—generally offer lower returns than
do securities with taxable returns. How can you tell when
it will pay to invest in municipals rather than in taxable
securities? This table provides some guidelines. For example, for an investor in the 31 percent tax bracket, a tax-free
return of 5 percent would be the equivalent of a taxable
return of 7.5 percent.

---

income tax. As you can see, the comparisons depend on what
your marginal (top) tax bracket is.

For example, if your top bracket is 31 percent, a return of 5
percent on a tax-exempt municipal is the equivalent of 7.25
percent on a similar security that's taxable. If the taxable security had a 7 percent return, you would be better off with a 5
percent municipal. On the other hand, if the taxable security
gave you a 7.5 percent return, that's a better deal.

To make these calculations yourself, you first express the
marginal tax bracket in decimal form—for example, .31

instead of 31 percent. Subtract that number from 1, which would give you .69 in this case. Then divide the tax-free return by that number. A 5 percent return would be the equivalent of 5 divided by .69, or 7.25 percent.

The table shows that the higher your tax bracket, the more likely it will pay to invest in tax-free municipals. But be sure to go through the calculations yourself before making any decisions. If you're in a low tax bracket, it probably won't be worth putting your money into municipals.

You should also consider state taxes. Although municipals are exempt from federal income tax, many of them are still subject to state income taxes. The exception is when the municipals are issued in your own state. In that case they're generally free of both federal and state taxes. A triple tax-free fund is one that's exempt from federal, state, and local income taxes.

If you're comparing a fund that invests in municipals with a fund that invests in similar securities subject to all three kinds of taxes (federal, state, and local), you'll have to base your calculations on your combined marginal tax rate. That is, you have to add the three rates together. Also, if you live in a high-tax area, your combined rate might reach 40 percent or more, which would make municipals more tempting. With a combined marginal rate of 40 percent, a 5 percent return on a municipal bond fund would be the equivalent of an 8.33 percent return on a corporate bond fund. (Divide 5 by .6.)

Geographic Divisions

Funds can be further classified as domestic; international or foreign; and global, which includes both U.S. and foreign stocks and bonds. Since these three kinds of funds tend to be out of phase with each other, it's a good idea to have your investments spread around geographically.

Families of Funds

Many investment companies operate several different funds. Fidelity Investments, for example, has about 200 different funds. The companies that operate many funds make it easy for you to switch back and forth between funds. But if you're following a buy-and-hold strategy, you'll want to avoid this kind of switching. Then, owning five funds operated by different companies makes just as much sense as owning five funds in the same family.

COSTS OF INVESTING

Investment costs vary widely from fund to fund, and it's tricky to figure out what an investor actually has to pay. There may be some up-front sales charges every time you put money into the fund, and there will surely be some annual charges. The fund may impose some charges when you withdraw cash. All of these charges can add up quickly. It pays to choose funds with fees that are relatively low.

Loads

Shares in mutual funds are sold several ways. Some are sold directly by the funds, some are sold by brokers or financial planners. Fund companies often add an *up-front load,* or sales charge, to pay salespeople. Naturally, the higher the commission, the greater the incentive for a salesperson to promote that particular fund. Sometimes, if a fund has proved to be very popular, the fund managers add a load to reward themselves. *Consumer Reports* has long recommended that readers avoid load funds and instead buy no-loads, which we'll explain shortly.

The maximum load is 8.5 percent. If you invested $1,000 in a fund with an 8.5 percent load, the fund would immediately subtract $85. So the amount you actually invest is $915.

A more practical way to look at this is to say, "I'm really investing $915 and paying a commission of $85. What does that come to as a percentage?" The answer is 9.3 percent. Any way you figure it, you're paying a lot to join the club.

Sometimes a fund has a sliding scale for its loads. If you invest $10,000, the load may be 8.5 percent. It might be less for the next $10,000. If you invest $1 million, your load may be practically zero.

Why would anyone invest in a fund with a load of 8.5 percent? The only time it makes sense is when the fund consistently provides a very high total return. And the only way you can work off the high initial expense is to hold the fund for several years. The higher the load, the longer you'll have to stay with the fund to work off the load.

Instead of a front-end load, some funds charge a *back-end load,* also known as a redemption fee, exit fee, or contingent deferred fee. This fee is imposed when you sell shares. The general idea is to provide an incentive to buy and hold. The load schedule is often set up so the back-end cost decreases the longer you hold the shares. For example, if you sell some of your shares a year after buying them, your load might be 5 percent. But after five or six years, the back-end load would disappear.

The advantage of a back-end load, as opposed to a front-end load, is that all of your money is invested immediately. If you invest $1,000, that money starts working for you right away. In the earlier example—$1,000 with a front-end load—you're working with an investment of only $915.

Many investment companies started out with funds loaded with an 8.5 percent sales charge, but competition has forced them to offer alternatives with smaller loads or no loads at all. On the other hand, some companies that started out with no-load funds have, as they assembled impressive track records, added loads to their most popular funds. One example is Fidelity's Magellan Fund, which started out as a no-load fund and now has a load of 3 percent.

Two-thirds of the 40 largest equity funds have loads ranging from 1 percent to the maximum. Half of these 40 funds have loads of 5 percent or more.

Do high-load funds perform better than low- or no-load funds? No. Why, then, are the top 40 stock funds so popular? Some simply have excellent track records, and their performance seems to justify the load. On the other hand, some of these funds have high loads and poor records, which suggests that they're popular mainly because they've been heavily promoted.

Ignore the sales pitch and concentrate on the performance record and the costs.

Load Versus No-Load Funds

Assuming its performance record is good, a no-load fund purchased directly from the investment company is your best buy. Many companies offer no-load funds with varying degrees of risk. Vanguard, for example, has more than a dozen no-load funds with risk ranging from low to very high. So it's possible to build a well-diversified portfolio including an array of no-load funds.

Annual Charges

All funds charge an annual fee for managing the fund. The fees are used to pay their staffs and cover trading costs. But because funds trade huge quantities of securities, their trading costs are proportionally much lower than they would be for an individual investor.

The basic annual fee is usually expressed as an expense ratio, which is a percentage of the fund's total value. The ratio can range anywhere from .25 percent to 2 percent. If you have $10,000 worth of shares in a fund, you can expect the fund to subtract between $25 and $200 each year in fees. Of course, the increase in the value of your investment should offset these annual costs.

Expense ratios vary widely, but each fund's ratio will usually be about the same from one year to the next. Some companies—Vanguard is again a prime example—have reputations for keeping their costs low.

You should also watch out for 12(b)-1 fees, which are named for the Securities and Exchange Commission (SEC) rule authorizing these fees. A fund can't charge them unless it states this intention in its prospectus. A fund that has a 12(b)-1 plan can charge an extra, annual fee of up to 1.25 percent of the value of the fund to cover marketing costs.

Don't be deceived by the apparently low charges. If you pay 1.25 percent a year on a $10,000 investment that grows 10 percent a year, at the end of 10 years you will have paid about $2,000 for 12(b)-1 fees.

More than half of the publicly available funds have 12(b)-1 charges. Obviously, it's a good idea to avoid these charges if you can. Look for real no-load funds: no front-end load, no back-end load, and no 12(b)-1 charges.

Starting in July 1993, the SEC has established new rules on mutual fund charges. The 12(b)-1 fees will be capped at 1 percent, and total sales charges will be capped at 7.25 percent.

GUIDELINES

1. **Diversify.** Don't put all your money in one fund. Buy several that have different characteristics, including different degrees of risk. A collection of high-, medium-, and low-risk funds will probably turn out to be less risky—and more profitable—than a collection of low-risk funds.
2. **Read each prospectus carefully.** It will give you the basics and warn you of problems.
3. **Buy funds that have good performance records.** Avoid new funds.
4. **Buy directly from the fund.** You don't need the advice of a broker or anyone else, and you don't need to pay a commission. Most funds have toll-free telephone numbers, which you can get by calling the toll-free directory at 800-555-1212.
5. **Buy no-load funds.** If you've already invested in a load fund, you might as well stay there. But your best buy in the future will be a fund that has no load at all and a small expense ratio. If you want to invest in a load fund that has a spectacular record, don't do so unless you're planning to hold the fund for several years.
6. **Keep a record of how much you've invested and on which dates.** That way, you can calculate your total returns over the years.

7. **Keep all the account statements supplied by the fund.**
   You'll need them for filing your tax return. The fund will
   withhold taxes on each year's income and capital gain,
   and it will supply a year-end summary.
8. **Review your funds' performance when the annual summaries are published, but don't worry about short-term
   calculations of changes in values.** If reading daily reports
   on mutual funds makes you nervous, you may be
   tempted to abandon your buy-and-hold strategy.

═ 7 ═

Your Home
as an Investment

Buying a house may be the best investment you'll ever make. It's also probably the riskiest investment—much more risky than buying stocks, for example. But the risk is usually justified by high rewards. If an individual or a family can afford it, a house should be at the center of the investment portfolio.

Why risky? You'll probably be assuming an enormous debt, and that can lead to trouble if something goes wrong with your financial plans—if you lose your job and can't find another one or you incur some very high medical bills. If you don't have enough set aside to cover these contingencies, and housing values are relatively low, you might have to sell your house at a loss.

How rewarding? If you choose the right property in the right location, there are great opportunities for capital gains. Even if you buy a property that appreciates slowly, the investment will provide tax advantages.

There are also other long-term advantages. One is that a house is usually a good hedge against inflation. For example, between 1970 and 1989, consumer prices tripled; during the same period, though, housing prices quadrupled. Of course, those were very good years for real estate, and it's impossible to predict whether that pattern will be repeated in the next 20 years.

Another advantage is that you can improve the returns on your investment by improving your property.

A third advantage: When you finance a house with a mortgage, part of each payment is allocated to your equity—the share of the house you own at any particular time. (See Table 4.1.) Equity building is really an automatic saving-and-investment plan.

TAX BREAKS

For many years, federal, state, and local governments have provided homeowners with some generous tax incentives.

Mortgage Interest

The current tax law allows you to deduct your mortgage interest payments from your taxable income. (Loans of $1 million or more aren't treated quite so favorably.) In chapter 4 we discussed how banks calculate interest payments and how you can calculate your tax savings by deducting those payments. In the example shown in Table 4.1, interest payments in the first year came to $8,973. All of that would be deductible from the buyer's income that year.

You can also deduct mortgage interest payments for a second home.

Property Tax

All property taxes are deductible expenses.

Capital Gains

If you sell a house for more than you paid for it, you'll have to pay income tax on the difference. But if you reinvest the entire amount in another house within two years, you won't have to pay tax on your gain until you sell that house. If you reinvest only part of your gain, you'll have to pay tax on the balance.

You can extend this tax benefit for as many houses as you

want. When you make your last sale, you'll have to pay tax on the gains you've accumulated throughout all of your transactions.

Once you've reached age 55, you're entitled to a one-time exclusion of up to $125,000 from your taxable gain. For example, if your cumulative gains reach $200,000, you'll have to pay tax on $75,000 when you make your final sale.

Caution: The break applies only to a primary residence that you've lived in for at least three of the last five years. And only one spouse is eligible for the break. If you use it, your spouse cannot.

IMPLICIT RENT

One of the hidden advantages of home ownership is that you, in effect, pay yourself rent for occupying the house. This is known as implicit rent or imputed rent. It's the equivalent of what you would receive if you were renting your house to someone else (minus operating expenses). This income is exempt from U.S. federal income tax but is taxable in many other countries, including the United Kingdom.

There's no need to calculate your implicit rent, but you should be aware that this is a real benefit to homeowners. In fact, the government includes estimates of implicit rent in its annual measures of the gross national product and the gross domestic product.

LEVERAGING

An important financial advantage of home ownership is that you can leverage your investment. That is, by putting a relatively small amount of money down, you can acquire a piece of property that's worth several times your original investment.

For example, suppose you buy a house priced at $100,000, and you put $20,000 down and finance the rest with a mortgage loan. Suppose, too, that your house increases in value by $5,000 in the first year, which is a modest return by historical standards. (Since 1947, the average return on unmortgaged residential real estate has been about 8 percent; as we'll see, returns on mortaged real estate are usually much higher.)

The question is, What's the return on your investment? The easy answer is 5 percent—$5,000 divided by $100,000. But as usual, the easy answer is wrong. It's wrong because your investment is $20,000, not $100,000. To calculate your return you divide the $5,000 by $20,000, which gives you a return of 25 percent. This is considerably higher than the expected returns on corporate stock. Nevertheless, this is a gross return. It has to be adjusted for the costs of investing in real estate (see below).

Leveraging substantially increases your return. The more you borrow to finance your purchase, the greater the leverage effect. Of course, the more you borrow, the greater the risk, too.

Table 7.1 illustrates the pluses and minuses of leveraging. It shows how leveraging works with an annual gain of $5,000 as compared with an annual loss of $5,000. It also shows how the leveraging effect works with down payments of 10, 20, and 30 percent.

Although leveraging can work to your disadvantage when housing values decline, remember that if the value of your property declines in any particular year, that's only a temporary loss. It's unimportant unless you're forced to sell when the market is down.

Does it ever make sense to pay 100 percent cash for your home? The answer depends on your attitude toward risk. If you pay cash, you avoid the risk of having to sell your home because you can't keep up the mortgage payments. Yet in the end, by avoiding the risk, you avoid the reward of a high return on investment. If you want to avoid real estate risk entirely, you should rent rather than buy.

ESTIMATING YOUR NET RETURN

Your gross return has to be adjusted for the costs of financing and maintaining the property. It should also be adjusted for

TABLE 7.1   HOW LEVERAGING WORKS

Example: House purchased for $100,000, with various down payments

	$10,000 DOWN	$20,000 DOWN	$30,000 DOWN	$40,000 DOWN
If the value increases $5,000 a year:				
Gross return on investment	50%	25%	17%	13%
If the value decreases $5,000 a year:				
Gross return on investment	−50%	−25%	−17%	−13%

One of the most important advantages of home ownership is that you can leverage your investment. That is, by putting a relatively small amount of money down, you can acquire a piece of property that's worth several times your original investment. Leveraging can also substantially increase your return on investment. Suppose you buy a $100,000 house for $20,000 down and finance the rest with a mortgage. If the value of the house increases by $5,000, that represents a 25 percent return on your original investment ($5,000 divided by $20,000). The catch is that leveraging also works in reverse. If your house declines in value by $5,000, that represents a negative return of 25 percent. This isn't a loss unless you have to sell the house at the lower price, but it does indicate how risky investing in real estate can be. However, in real estate as in other investments, returns are generally parallel to risk.

---

tax saving because of the deductibility of interest payments and property taxes. And last, it should be adjusted for implicit rental income.

Table 7.2 shows how to make these adjustments. This is necessarily a crude analysis because, in practice, many of the estimates would be guesses. It's not necessary to try to make these calculations yourself, but you should understand the factors at work.

TABLE 7.2 HOW TO FIGURE YOUR NET RETURN

Situation: A house purchased for $100,000 is worth $105,000 at the end of the first year.
Question: What's the return on investment?
Answer: Depends on how the purchase was financed.
Three cases considered in this example:
1. Cash purchase
2. $20,000 down payment and a 30-year, $80,000 mortgage at 9 percent
3. $20,000 down payment and a 30-year, $80,000 mortgage at 7 percent

	CASH PURCHASE	9 PERCENT MORTGAGE	7 PERCENT MORTGAGE
Initial investment	$100,000	$20,000	$20,000
Gross increase in value	5,000	5,000	5,000
Minus annual cost of maintaining property			
Interest payment	0	7,178	6,387
Property tax	1,000	1,000	1,000
Insurance	500	500	500
Maintenance, repairs, heating	1,500	1,500	1,500
Gross cost	$ 3,000	$10,178	$ 9,387
Tax saving on interest and property tax (33% tax bracket)	330	2,699	2,438
Net cost	2,670	7,479	6,949

118

Plus implicit rent	6,000	6,000	6,000
Equals net return	8,330	3,521	4,051
Return on investment	8%	18%	20%

Homeowners tend to underestimate the value of owning a home. The homeowner who chooses the right house in the right location can end up with an extraordinarily profitable investment. It's hard to estimate the return on real estate because some of the key contributing factors are obscure—leveraging, tax breaks, and implicit rent.

Leveraging: As Table 7.1 shows, the more you borrow to finance your purchase, the higher your potential return. The table above compares an all-cash purchase with purchases financed with mortgages at two different interest rates. *Tax breaks:* Since interest costs and property taxes are deductible from your taxable income, they have an important effect on net return. They must be subtracted from gross maintenance costs. *Implicit rent:* This is the rent you in effect pay yourself. It's what you would have to pay a landlord if you were renting the house. Implicit rent is actually untaxed income and should be considered part of your return on investment. *Net return:* This is what's left after you've accounted for the appreciation in property value, maintenance costs, tax breaks, and implicit rent. In this conservative example, the net return for those who leveraged their investment is well above the expected return for corporate stocks.

This procedure can be used to figure the net return in any particular year. Closing costs have been ignored because they occur only in the first year.

— 8 —

Systems
for Saving

Start a saving program as soon as you have that first job. Automatic payroll saving programs are better than discretionary saving programs. Tax-deductible programs are the best of all.

TAX CONSEQUENCES

Some retirement plans are tax-deductible and some are tax-deferred.

With *tax-deductible* plans, the money you contribute to your retirement fund can be deducted from your taxable income. For example, if you contribute $5,000 to a fund, that $5,000 can be subtracted from your taxable income for the year. That saves you roughly $1,650 in income tax. An additional advantage is that the earnings on that contribution accumulate tax-free until you begin making withdrawals.

With *tax-deferred* plans, you can't deduct your contribution from your taxable income. Your contribution will consist of already-taxed dollars. But the earnings accumulate tax-free until you begin making withdrawals.

The money you contribute to either type of plan can be invested in a variety of ways—in a mutual fund, for example. Your investment choices will depend on your risk preferences and the options your employer offers. If it's not an employer-sponsored program, you can make your own choices. Avoid investing in tax-free municipals, because your earnings will accumulate tax-free anyway.

There are many restrictions on how your money can be contributed and withdrawn. The primary rule is that the law prohibits the withdrawal of any of your contribution until you reach age 59½. If you withdraw all or part of your fund before that time, you have to pay a 10 percent penalty (unless you meet hardship requirements). You don't have to withdraw any of your fund until you reach 70½. At that point, you will have to make periodic withdrawals. The annual amount you must withdraw depends on the size of your fund at age 70½ and how many years you're expected to live. If you don't withdraw enough on schedule, you'll have to pay a 50 percent penalty.

TRENDS IN PENSION PLANS

Corporations and other organizations that offer pension plans are making significant changes in the form of their plans. They're gradually shifting from defined-benefit to defined-contribution plans.

Defined-benefit Plans

These plans are usually financed entirely by your employer. When you retire, you collect a fixed amount every month until you die. The amount depends on how many years you were employed and how much you earned.

For the employer, this kind of plan can be expensive. If you retire at 65 and live another 20 years, the employer has to carry that expense for those years. But inflation will erode the payments year after year, which presents a problem for the employee. The payments are fixed, but the purchasing power of those dollars will decline.

Say the inflation rate is 4 percent a year. A monthly payment that begins at $1,000 will decline, in real dollars (dollars adjusted for inflation), to $960 the second year, to $922 the third year, to $885 the fourth year, and so on.

Chart 8.1 shows how inflation can reduce the value of a fixed payment. Let's assume that your nominal payment (in dollars not adjusted for inflation) is $20,000 a year. If you had started receiving that payment in 1970, by 1990 its real value (in dollars adjusted for inflation) would have been approximately $5,000. The 1970–1990 period happened to have a fairly high average rate of inflation. But even with a low rate of inflation, the value of a fixed income is bound to decline substantially over the years.

If you are covered by a pension plan to which both you and your employer contribute, and you leave the company, you can take all of the money you've contributed. You may be able to take some or all of the money your employer contributed. How much you can take will depend on your former employer's vesting schedule, which shows how many years it takes for you to have full rights of ownership of the fund. Say your employer's plan specifies that you will be partially vested for the first four years of your employment—20 percent the first year, 40 percent the second, 60 percent the third, and 80 percent the fourth—and fully vested at the end of the fifth year. If you leave the company at the end of the first year, you'll be able to take only 20 percent of the amount contributed for you. If you leave after the fifth year, you can take the entire amount.

If you change jobs throughout your career, and leave before you're fully vested, you will collect a smaller pension than if you had stayed with one company for 20 or 30 years (which is becoming more and more difficult to do). If you make a career move, be sure to check with the company's employee-benefits office to find out what's due you.

Defined-benefit plans are covered by the Pension Benefit Guaranty Corporation in case the employer goes broke. But the coverage is limited. There is a maximum payment ad-

Inflation is a serious problem for someone who retires with a fixed income, such as a pension that provides the same dollar amount of income from one year to the next. This chart shows how a retiree's real pension income would have been eroded by inflation in the years between 1970 and 1990. If someone retired with a $20,000 annual income in 1970, that income would have been effectively reduced to about $5,000 by 1990. The retiree would still be receiving $20,000 a year, but by 1990 that money would buy only about a quarter of the amount of goods and services that would have been available for $20,000 in 1970.

CHART 8.1 HOW INFLATION ERODES THE REAL VALUE OF A $20,000 PENSION, 1970–90

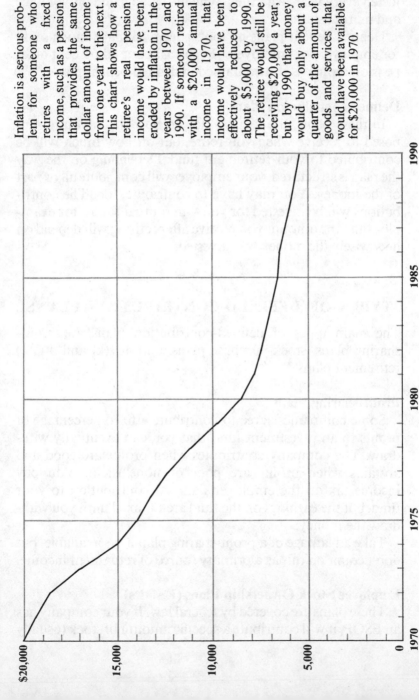

justed every year. And the payments will depend on your age and marital status.

Defined-benefit plans no longer seem to make much sense for employers or employees. Even so, about 80 percent of all pension money is still contained in defined-benefit plans.

Defined-contribution Plans

In these plans, the focus is not on how much you're supposed to receive when you retire, but on how much will be contributed to your retirement fund. Depending on the way the plan is structured, your employer will contribute all or part of the money. You may have to contribute, too. The contributions will be invested for you—in mutual funds, for example—and the amount you receive after retiring will depend on how wisely the money was invested.

TYPES OF DEFINED-CONTRIBUTION PLANS

The main types of defined-contribution plans are profit-sharing plans, stock-purchase plans, and 401(k) and 403(b) retirement plans.

Profit-sharing Plans

Some companies agree to contribute a fixed percentage of profits to an investment fund that you can eventually withdraw. The company contributes when profits are good and abstains when profits are poor or nonexistent. You pay income tax on the employer's annual contribution to your fund, but the earnings on the fund aren't taxed until you withdraw the money.

Take advantage of a profit-sharing plan if it's available, but don't count on this as a primary source of retirement income.

Employee Stock Ownership Plans (ESOPs)

These plans are covered by federal law. If your company has an ESOP, it will contribute a specific amount of stock (usually the company's own stock) to a fund for your use. When you leave the company, you may collect either the number of shares in your fund or the cash equivalent of the value of those shares, which is treated as taxable income upon withdrawal.

Caution: You can't be sure you'll collect anything; the company may declare bankruptcy or go out of business. It's also sometimes difficult to determine the worth of the stock. If the stock is publicly traded, you can usually find out its value by checking the newspapers. If the stock isn't available to the public, the value will be estimated by an agent of the company. You can't be sure the estimate is accurate.

You should be aware of a couple of options required by law. If you've been in the plan for 10 years or more and reach age 55, you can request that 25 percent of your fund be invested in assets other than stock in the company. Five years later, you can request that half of the remaining company stock be switched to other assets. It's a good idea to take advantage of these options to diversify your investment.

You should think of an ESOP fund as a supplementary fund. You'll obviously have to rely mainly on an investment plan that you can control yourself.

401(k) and 403(b) Plans

These are good deals. They're tax-deductible programs financed by voluntary payroll deductions. The names refer to the sections of the law authorizing these programs; 401(k) plans are generally for employees of for-profit corporations, and 403(b) plans are generally for not-for-profit organizations. The main difference is that you can contribute (in 1992) up to $8,728 a year to a 401(k) plan and $9,500 to a 403(b) plan. These maximums change from time to time.

Employers sometimes make contributions to these funds. For example, your employer might match half of the amount you contribute up to, say, 6 percent of your income. That is, if you contribute 6 percent of your income to your fund, your employer will contribute an additional 3 percent. You end up with a 9 percent contribution.

Depending on how the plan is set up, you may also be able to contribute money on which you've paid tax. In addition to the basic contribution of $8,728, you might want to contribute $3,000, for instance. The total contribution, including what the company pays, is limited to 25 percent of your annual net income (after subtracting your payroll contribution). There's also an annual dollar limit: $30,000. The advantage of making the extra contribution is that the earnings on that investment will accumulate tax-free until you withdraw the money.

Most companies allow employees to borrow from the plan for certain purposes. Your investment keeps working for you, and you borrow at the current interest rates. This kind of loan may be useful for financing a college education. But since the interest payments usually aren't tax-deductible, you may want to consider the alternative of a home equity loan, where the interest payments *are* deductible.

Keep your money in a tax-deductible program if you move to another company. You may have a few options: leaving the money in the fund sponsored by the previous company, transferring it into a similar fund at your new company, or transferring it into an Individual Retirement Account (IRA). Legally, you'll have 60 days to make the arrangements.

If you have an opportunity to participate in one of these plans, contribute as much as you can.

RETIREMENT PLANS
FOR THE SELF-EMPLOYED

These plans are also good deals. They're designed for people who are fully or partly self-employed. If you have an employer and have your own business on the side, you can participate in your employer's 401(k) plan and contribute to a separate savings plan at home.

Keogh Plans

These are named after the sponsor of the legislation authorizing this form of saving. Four versions are currently available:

- *The profit-sharing Keogh.* This is the most flexible version. You can contribute up to 15 percent of your annual net income (revenue minus expenses, including the Keogh contribution itself), with a ceiling of $30,000. You don't have to contribute the full amount, and you don't have to contribute every year. But the amount you contribute is tax-deductible. Mutual funds, banks, savings-and-loan associations, and stockbrokers can help you set up a plan to invest your money as you choose.
- *The money-purchase Keogh.* This plan follows a rigid set of rules. You have to decide what percentage of your income you want to contribute, and you have to contribute that amount every year. You can contribute up to 25 percent of your net income, with a maximum of $30,000. Again, the contributions are tax-deductible. If you don't contribute the full amount you've agreed to contribute, you'll have to pay a penalty. So this plan should be avoided unless you're sure you can contribute the same amount of cash every year.
- *The combination Keogh.* This allows you to use both of the first two versions. You agree to contribute, say, 15 percent of your income to a money-purchase Keogh. If you want to contribute the maximum of 25 percent, you can put another 10 percent in a profit-sharing Keogh. That way, you'll have the option of contributing as little as 15 percent a year or as much as 25 percent.
- *The defined-benefit Keogh.* This plan is cumbersome and expensive to administer, but it may help you accumulate a substantial pension fund. You decide when you want to retire and how much annual income you would like to receive after retirement. Your annual contributions before retirement will be calculated by an actuary, a specialist who estimates how long you can be expected to live and how much you'll have to contribute to cover the cost of supplying your annual pension payments. The contributions have to be recalculated every year, and you will have to pay the actuary to make those recalculations. This

plan is appropriate only for people who have high incomes and expect to retire in 10 years or so. As with all defined-benefit plans, it's quite likely that the value of your annual income after retirement will be seriously eroded by inflation.

Keogh plans can be complicated if you employ other people. They have to be covered by the plan, too. Check with an accountant before you decide whether and how you want to set up a plan for yourself and your employees.

Simplified Employee Pension Plans (SEPs)

These plans are similar to profit-sharing Keoghs. The same contribution limits apply, and you don't have to contribute unless you want to. But SEPs are much simpler to set up and control. They have many of the characteristics of an IRA.

INDIVIDUAL RETIREMENT ACCOUNTS (IRAs)

An IRA is a retirement plan you establish with a custodian approved by the Internal Revenue Service—a mutual fund, credit union, bank, or insurance company, for example. You can contribute up to $2,000 a year. In two-income families, each partner can contribute $2,000. In one-income families, the wage earner can contribute an extra $250 on behalf of his or her spouse.

As with a 401(k) plan, the earnings on your investment are tax-deferred. You can't withdraw any of your funds until you reach age 59½, or you will incur a penalty.

Your IRA contribution may be tax-deductible under certain circumstances: neither you nor your spouse (if you're married) is eligible to participate in any company retirement plan, *or* your adjusted gross income is less than $25,000 ($40,000 in the case of a two-income family). If your income is higher than that, you can have a partial deduction.

If you leave a company and collect tax-deductible or tax-deferred funds in a lump sum, you can transfer that money into an IRA. But make it a separate IRA. Don't add that money into an existing IRA; you may have trouble keeping track of your funds for tax purposes.

MANAGING YOUR RETIREMENT FUNDS

As noted earlier, the trend in retirement plans is toward those that leave it up to the employee to decide how the contributions are to be invested, within limits specified by the sponsoring organization. About 40 million American working people are eligible to participate in such employee-directed plans.

How well do these employees manage their money? Not very well. Many who are eligible for these plans don't bother to participate. Those who do participate tend to invest their money very cautiously, which seriously reduces their potential retirement income.

For example, although employees commonly have the option of investing in an equity mutual fund, three-fourths of these workers ignore stocks completely. Only 4 percent have at least half of their money in stocks.

About 60 percent of the money in these self-directed plans is in the form of *guaranteed investment contracts,* or GICs. These contracts are issued by insurance companies. (Banks offer similar contracts called BICs.) You invest a certain amount of money for a certain period of time—usually from one to five years—and your fund receives a fixed amount of interest, which remains tax-free until you withdraw it. The value of your investment is constant. At the end of the contract, the money can be reinvested in a new contract or switched to some other form of investment.

GICs resemble bank certificates of deposit in that the value of the investment doesn't change during the term of the contract, and the interest rate is fixed. Since GIC money is usually invested in Treasury securities, the returns are close to those of CDs with similar maturities.

However, these investments aren't insured, and if the insurance company goes out of business, you could lose your investment. So far, this hasn't been a problem. But because some large corporations are concerned about it, they've removed GICs from the list of choices for employee investments.

Tax-deferred annuities are also used by many people to save for retirement. These too are insurance company contracts, though they're available from several sources—insurance agents, brokers, bankers, financial planners, and mutual funds. Most people use annuities to provide regular income after retirement. You contribute money either in a lump sum or through periodic payments, and then make withdrawals when you need the money.

In a way, these annuities work like IRAs: The earnings on your contribution accumulate tax-free. Once you reach age 59½, you can begin withdrawing money. The main difference between the two is that your contribution isn't limited to $2,000 a year. You can invest many thousands of dollars.

The standard contract is called a *fixed annuity.* You earn a specific amount of interest for a specific amount of time, usually a year. The rate is adjusted every year in line with current money market rates, so it's not really fixed. There are many traps and complications for those who invest in annuities, and the costs vary a lot. A useful list of companies with competitive rates is included in the *Annuity Shopper,* published by United States Annuities, 98 Hoffman Road, Englishtown, NJ 07726. The cost is $20 plus $4 for shipping and handling. The telephone number is 800-872-6684.

The only way to build a healthy retirement fund is to invest a substantial portion of your money in corporate stock. The value of your stock investments will fluctuate, but over the long term no other investment in securities will serve you better. Your expected returns will be relatively high, and inflation will be a minor threat. As you grow older and your need for current income increases, you can change your mix of stocks—from growth stocks to income-producing stocks, for example. But your retirement fund will perform better for you if you focus on stocks as long as you can.

On the other hand, if you reach your sixties and put most of your money into fixed-income investments, inflation will erode much of that fund during the next 10 or 20 years. That is *not* playing it safe.

SOCIAL SECURITY RETIREMENT BENEFITS

The rules of Social Security are sometimes complicated, and they continue to change. Here are some essentials you should know.

Who Qualifies?

For most people, 10 years' worth of Social Security tax payments will qualify them for retirement benefits.

When Can You Start Collecting Benefits?

If you were born before 1938, you can collect full benefits at age 65. But the standard retirement age is rising. For example, if you were born after 1959, you'll have to wait until you're 67 to collect full benefits.

Those who were born before 1938 can begin collecting reduced benefits at 62. But as of this writing, your benefits will be only 80 percent of the full amount available to you at age 65. (This will be reduced to 70 percent for people born after 1938.) So it pays to postpone collecting Social Security benefits until you reach the designated retirement age for people in your age group.

If you further postpone your retirement, you'll get a bonus of up to 8 percent per year until you reach age 70. (The bonus will depend on the calendar year when you retire.) Then the government will start sending you checks whether you're retired or not.

There are many factors to consider in deciding when to retire—your health, your expected life span, your total income, your spouse's age, whether your spouse has paid Social Security taxes, and so on. Check with a Social Security expert before you make a decision. The Social Security Administration (SSA) has approximately 1,300 local offices; consult your phone directory under "United States Government Offices." Or call SSA's Washington office: 800-772-1213. While you're inquiring about your account, ask for the booklet *Understanding Social Security*.

How Much Can You Collect?

That depends on how much you've paid in over the years. If you've paid the maximum Social Security tax every year, you collect the maximum benefits. The maximums are adjusted every year to keep up with inflation. Right now, if you were born in the 1930s and paid the maximum for 10 years, your full benefits may be up to $1,000 a month. If you and your spouse are about the same age and both paid the maximum for 10 years, each of you could collect full benefits.

You can get more precise estimates by calling the Social Security Administration to find out what your benefits would be if you were 65 and retired this year. The SSA can't estimate what your benefits might be if you were to retire a few years from now, because the benefits change every year. If you want a detailed personal report on how much money was paid into the system and how much you're likely to receive in retirement, ask for Form SSA-7004-PC. Complete the form and return it, and you will receive a Personal Earnings and Benefit Estimate Statement. If you find any errors in the statement, be sure to report them to the SSA.

Retirement Benefits for Spouses

If one spouse has a Social Security account and the other doesn't, the second spouse is eligible for benefits equal to 50 percent of the first spouse's benefit, as long as that spouse is living. If the first spouse dies, the second spouse's benefit increases to 100 percent of the first spouse's benefit.

Penalties for Working After Retirement

If you retire at any point between the ages of 62 and 70, you may be penalized for working. There are limits on how much you can earn as an employee or as a self-employed person, and these limits are adjusted every year.

The penalities depend on the age at which you retire. If you are under 65 when you retire, you can earn up to $7,440 per year and still collect all of your Social Security benefits. But for every $2 you earn over that limit, $1 will be withheld from your benefits.

If your retirement age is between 65 and 69, you can earn up to $10,200 per year and still collect all of your Social Security benefits. But for every $3 you earn over that limit, $1 will be withheld from your benefits.

Taxes

Until you reach 70, you'll have to consider the possibility of paying tax on your Social Security benefits. Normally, Social Security benefits aren't subject to federal income tax until you reach a certain income level: $25,000 for single persons and $32,000 for married couples. Some states also impose a tax on Social Security benefits.

The calculations are different from those for regular income tax. You begin with *half* of your Social Security income. Then you add all of your other kinds of income: wages, dividends, pensions, interest (including interest from municipal securities). If this total exceeds the limit, you have to pay tax on 50 percent of the excess or 50 percent of the benefits, whichever is less.

Keep in mind, too, that as long as you're working for someone else or for yourself, you're required to pay Social Security tax.

Other Benefits

There are special benefits for blind and disabled workers and their families, and for low-income families. Everyone over the age of 65 is entitled to Medicare benefits.

GUIDELINES

1. **Invest as much as you can in tax-favored plans.** But don't depend entirely on these plans. Be sure to build up a sep-

arate retirement fund as a backup. Mutual funds are your best bet.

2. **If you want to build a healthy fund, concentrate on stocks instead of fixed-income investments.** That way, you can be reasonably sure that your annual returns exceed the inflation rate by a comfortable margin.

3. **Arrange to have your saving done automatically.** That removes most of the agony of saving.

4. **Own your own home.** Your house represents a large investment fund. You can speed up the growth of that fund by paying off your mortgage ahead of time.

= 9 =

Passing Your Property to Others

WHY YOU NEED A WILL

Actually, you have a will whether you want one or not. If you die without a will that you've tailored for your own purposes, your state will give you a one-size-fits-all will. And the results may not be exactly what you had in mind.

The state, through a probate or surrogate court, will appoint an administrator to handle the distribution of your assets. That will take time and money, to be subtracted from your assets. The laws of your state may require that your assets be divided in a way you wouldn't have approved. And if you have minor dependents, the state will appoint a guardian, again one that you might not have approved.

A will makes certain your property is distributed the way you want, with a minimum of delay and expense. It also gives you a chance to appoint an appropriate guardian for minors.

The time to prepare your first will is when you've acquired some assets that can be passed on to someone else, or when you've acquired minor dependents. If you're married, your spouse should also have a will. If you're not married but you're half of a couple in a permanent relationship, it's extremely important to have a will. Otherwise the law won't recognize the arrangement.

There are a few eligibility requirements: You have to be above a certain age (14 to 21, depending on the state), you must be fully aware of the consequences of making a will, and you must act voluntarily.

Your will doesn't have to be complicated. President Calvin Coolidge squeezed his will into a single sentence: "I leave my entire estate to my wife, Grace, and request that she be appointed executrix without bond." Your will might be that simple. But chances are that you'll have more than one beneficiary, and you should be specific about who gets what, when, and under what circumstances.

Your will should answer three basic questions: Who should settle your financial affairs? Who should take care of your minor children? How should your property be distributed?

WHAT YOU'LL HAVE TO DECIDE

Executors

You'll have to select the person who's going to assemble your property, inventory it, pay your debts, pay your funeral expenses, file estate and income tax returns, pay any taxes due, sell property if necessary to meet your obligations, distribute the remaining property according to your will, and submit a final accounting to your beneficiaries and the probate court. Of course, your executor can get help from a lawyer or an accountant.

Trustees

A trust is a fund or some other form of property held by one party for the benefit of another. It's a device for avoiding estate taxes. In that case, you'll want to appoint a trustee—someone to manage the trust, perhaps with the help of a lawyer. The trustee and the executor can be the same person.

If you want to put a substantial amount of money in trust, a bank can be appointed trustee. But they may charge several thousand dollars a year. Some banks won't handle a trust unless it amounts to several thousand dollars.

Guardians

You should appoint a guardian for any minor children in your family. If you have a large estate, you should probably appoint two guardians, a personal guardian and a property guardian. The personal guardian would take the place of a parent in raising the child. The property guardian would handle the child's inheritance, giving the personal guardian as much money as necessary to take care of the child. The property guardian might be a lawyer or a financial expert, and the personal guardian should be a family member or a close friend of the parents.

Fees

When someone dies intestate, or without a will, state law usually sets a maximum fee for a court-appointed administrator. It's usually a small percentage of the value of the estate, subtracted before the property is distributed to beneficiaries. Your executor is entitled to a similar fee, unless you state otherwise in your will.

Bonds

Unless the will states otherwise, executors, trustees, and guardians are required to post bonds. The bond is based on the value of the property to be managed, and a premium is paid annually as an estate expense until the job is done. Most wills state that such bonds aren't necessary.

How to Divide Your Property

Your will covers all property that isn't covered by other documents. For example, if you and your spouse are recorded as the joint owners of your home or other property, you don't have to mention those properties in your will.

You can make specific and general gifts. An example of a *specific gift:* You leave your antique sports car to a particular child or friend. *General gifts:* You leave, say, $5,000 to each of

CHART 9.1   A SIMPLE WILL

I, John Smith, of 333 Main Street, Des Moines, Iowa, declare and publish that this is my last will, revoking all previous wills.
1. Executors. I appoint my wife, Mary Smith, executor of this will. I also appoint my friend, Richard Jones, substitute executor, in case Mary is unable or unwilling to act as executor, or ceases to do so. The executor does not have to be bonded or file other security for the performance of his or her duties.
2. Guardians. If Mary dies before I do, or at the same time, I appoint my sister, Barbara James, guardian of the persons and property of my children until they are eighteen (18) years old. I also appoint my brother, William Smith, substitute guardian, in case Barbara is unable or unwilling to act as guardian, or ceases to do so. The guardian does not have to be bonded or file other security for the performance of his or her duties.
3. Specific bequests. I give my MG sports car to my son, Robert Smith. If he dies before I do, or at the same time, this car is to become part of my residuary estate. I give my Picasso etching to my daughter, Jane Smith. If she dies before I do, or at the same time, this etching is to become part of my residuary estate.
4. General bequests. I give my children, Robert and Jane, three thousand dollars ($3,000) each. If either dies before I do, or at the same time, his or her gift is to become part of my residuary estate.
5. Residuary estate. I give all the rest of my property and any

---

a dozen friends or organizations. Your executor will have to withdraw that money from your bank account. If there's not enough, the executor will have to sell some of the property.

The executor will pay all of your debts, administrative expenses, and taxes. After these expenses have been paid and the specific and general gifts have been distributed, the balance is called the *residuary estate.* You can have that property dis-

lapsed bequests to my wife, Mary. If she dies before I do, or at the same time, I give all of this property to my children, Robert and Jane, in equal parts. If all three of these people die before I do, or at the same time, all my property is to go to my sister, Barbara, and my brother, William, in equal parts, or entirely to the sole survivor if only one outlives me.

6. Taxes. All taxes and government fees associated with the transfer of my property are to be paid out of the residuary estate.

7. Executor's powers. In order to carry out the administration and distribution of my estate, I give my executor full power to sell, lease, mortgage, reinvest, or otherwise dispose of the assets in my estate.

Signed: _____

Date: _____

Witnesses. At John Smith's request, we met on the date inserted above to witness his signing of this will. With all of us present at the same time, he signed it and stated it was his last will and asked us to sign it as witnesses to it.

Signed: _____ Address: _____

Signed: _____ Address: _____

Signed: _____ Address: _____

SOURCE: *Consumer Reports*, July 1980.

---

tributed just about any way you wish, but the law usually specifies a minimum amount to be left to your spouse.

Suppose you stated that you wanted to leave 25 percent to your spouse but the law required that your spouse receive 50 percent if you die without a will. In that case, your spouse can request that the court override the will and award him or her 50 percent of the property.

DO YOU NEED A LAWYER?

Chart 9.1 is an example of a simple will. It's not absolutely necessary to hire a lawyer to draft your will, but it's a good idea to do so if your estate is complex. The cost will vary according to the complexity. You may be able to hold the cost down by doing most of the homework before you see the lawyer. Conduct a complete inventory of your property and valuable papers, make an estimate of your net worth, and be sure to have all the records for any property you own jointly. Make tentative decisions about beneficiaries, executors, guardians, and such.

WHEN IT'S USEFUL TO HIRE A LAWYER

If you want to set up a trust. This requires some careful planning. Don't make any decisions until you talk with an expert.

If you're planning to disinherit someone. Wills are sometimes challenged by people who would otherwise be beneficiaries if there were no will. It's important to make sure that your will is specific about persons to be excluded.

If one of the beneficiaries needs special care. For example, you might make detailed arrangements for a disabled child.

If you have property complications. Perhaps you own a small business and you want to arrange for one of your beneficiaries to assume control. The details will have to spelled out clearly.

EVALUATING YOUR ESTATE

You probably have a bigger estate than you think. You can estimate by using the net worth form (a summary of your assets minus liabilities) in Worksheet 1.1. List any property you own singly or as a co-owner—for example, a small business.

Include anything that's payable to your estate. For instance, you can make your life insurance payable to your estate. However, if you retain any control over your insurance—if you can cancel the policy or change the beneficiary—it's still your property and should be included in your estate. If your employer pays for an insurance policy on your life, that's handled differently. If you make your spouse or another family member the owner of the policy, then the proceeds won't be part of your estate.

Record the value of your property according to its fair market value—what you could sell it for. You should probably try to be accurate about this, to get some idea of whether you're going to encounter problems with estate tax. But your property will be formally appraised when you die.

FORMS OF OWNERSHIP

The way you own your property can affect the way your estate is taxed.

Variations in State Law

Some states have a community property system and others a common law system. In the states that have a community property system—Arizona, California, Idaho, Louisiana, Nevada, New Mexico, Texas, and Washington—it's generally assumed that a husband and wife each own half of all property acquired during their marriage, except inherited property and gifts from third parties to one spouse and not the other. But the definitions differ from state to state, and you should consult a lawyer to see what should be included in your estate.

The common law system applies in all other states. That means a husband and wife separately own whatever they've independently purchased with their own money. If one spouse has no income, it's assumed the other is the owner of all property acquired during the marriage.

Whose Name Is on the Title or Deed?

If more than one name appears on the document of ownership, the property is jointly owned. There are two main forms of joint ownership—joint tenancy and tenancy in common.

When you have *joint tenancy,* also known as joint tenancy with right of survivorship, the survivor gets the property when one dies. If you have a joint tenancy, the property should not be included in your will.

With a *tenancy in common,* each owner's share goes to his or her heirs instead of the survivor. For example, you and three friends each own a quarter share in a commercial building. If you die, your share will go to your family, or to whomever you designate in your will.

A third form of ownership, *tenancy* by the entirety, is like a joint tenancy, but it applies only to real estate owned by a husband and wife. When one dies, the other automatically acquires the property.

It's very important to keep records of how jointly owned property was acquired. You must be able to supply proof that each co-owner put up part of the purchase money or acquired his or her share as a gift or an inheritance. Otherwise, the Internal Revenue Service will assume that the entire value of jointly owned property should be included in the estate of the co-owner who dies first.

Recording Jointly Owned Property
on Your Net Worth Statement

Here's how to treat the various possibilities:

- *Community property.* If you're married and live in a community property state, your list of assets should include only half the value of each item acquired during your marriage. If any piece of property is tied to a mortgage or some other form of debt, only half of the unpaid balance should be included in your list of liabilities. Anything you own separately should be recorded at full market value.
- *Inherited or gift property.* If you and two siblings own some stock inherited from your parents, include only 33 percent of the value on your net worth statement.
- *Property bought by you and other owners.* If you and a

friend bought a boat for $10,000 and you put up $7,500, you should record your share as 75 percent of the boat's current market value.

• *Property owned by a husband and wife.* Even though one spouse contributed most or all of the money to buy a piece of property, the law allows you to assume that each spouse owns half. But the primary contributor has to file a form indicating that he or she has made a gift to the spouse. If you've filed the papers, your list of assets should include half of the current market value of the property.

AVOIDING TAXES

The federal government taxes large estates and large gifts. Many states impose similar taxes. But there are ample opportunities to avoid paying anything at all.

You can leave as much as you want to your spouse, and it won't be subject to estate tax. However, when he or she dies, that part of his or her estate exceeding $600,000 will be subject to income tax. If your spouse remarries, he or she can pass the entire estate on to the new spouse without being subject to estate tax.

Quite apart from what you leave your spouse, you can leave up to $600,000 to any other person or group of people without paying estate tax. If you go over the $600,000 limit, the excess will be taxed at the rate of 37 percent. That rate applies to the first $3 million above $600,000. The rate jumps to 55 percent after that.

So if you're not wealthy, you can probably avoid estate taxes without resorting to special arrangements. But if your estate is fairly large, you should consider some of the available tax-avoidance maneuvers. Consult with a lawyer before you follow through.

Give Money Away

One way to reduce your taxable estate is to make periodic gifts to your family or friends or anyone else. You can give up to $10,000 a year to any number of people without running into a tax problem. If your spouse joins in, you can give up to $20,000 to each friend or relative tax-free. There are no limits on gifts between spouses.

If you do give someone more than $10,000, you'll have to file a tax return notifying the Internal Revenue Service. But you don't have to pay a tax right away, if ever. The IRS keeps track of these excessive gifts and adds them to the value of your estate when you die. Still, this applies only to that part of your estate that isn't being left to your spouse. If that part is worth $600,000 or less, you pay no tax.

All contributions to charities—money or property—are tax-free.

Give Your Insurance Policy Away

Give your policy to your spouse, to your children, or to a trust. The new owner must have full control over the policy and pay the premiums.

Avoid Inheritances

If you have plenty of money already and someone leaves you more in the form of an inheritance, you can decline to accept it. The money will then go to your heirs. That way, it never enters your estate and isn't subject to estate tax.

Set up a Bypass Trust

There are many different kinds of trusts, but this is one of the most useful. It works only when each spouse owns substantial property separately. If your home is your main asset and you own it jointly, there won't be much separately owned property to be concered about.

How a Bypass Trust Works

You establish it through your will or a separate document, and nominate a trustee or team of trustees. You turn over a sizable amount of money—up to $600,000—to the trust with the provision that it will be passed on to your children when your spouse dies. The trustee invests the money, and the spouse receives the earnings from that investment. If necessary, the spouse can extract the principal. In other words, all of the trust money is available to your spouse, but it's bequeathed to your children. When your spouse dies, all of the remaining trust money automatically goes to the children, tax-free.

Your money (or property) escapes estate taxes twice: once when you turn it over to the trust, and once when your spouse dies and the money is transferred to your children. The spouse's estate will be separate, and he or she can leave the children up to $600,000 tax-free.

Appendix

FAMILY FINANCE WORKBOOK

INTRODUCTION

Most families today have the same financial goals: day-to-day monetary security, funds for children's education, enough money for comfortable retirement. Yet few families feel confident that they can meet all these goals. Certainly many people try at one time or another to stick to a budget, but the tendency of wage earners is to spend more than they make, a situation often worsened by an excessive reliance on credit.

True, unless you inherit a fortune or win the lottery, you'll probably have to realize your financial goals with only your salary and benefits. But you *can* use your income more effectively, and redirect money toward some long-term goals, by taking a good hard look at your family's expenditures. Become aware of your spending and saving habits, understand where your discretionary income lies, and then establish a realistic financial plan for the future.

This workbook, if used properly, can help you get out of debt, reorganize your financial priorities, and work toward your immediate and long-term goals.

How to Use the Worksheets

This workbook is divided into three parts. The worksheets in Parts I and II—"Where Your Money Is Now: Current Expenses" and "Taking Stock of Your Family's Finances: Current Assets"—help you see your family's current financial picture. When you complete these worksheets, you will know exactly where your money is today and how you are spending it. Many of these worksheets will also help you keep track of important financial information, such as payment dates and premiums for life insurance policies, and make you aware of the annual percentage rates you pay for the privilege of using credit cards. The worksheets in Part III—Where You Want

149

Your Money to Go: Financial Goals—are designed to help you redirect your family's spending, set goals, devise new monthly and yearly spending plans, and identify new sources of investment savings.

Dissecting and budgeting the family finances may not be fun, but one or two weekends spent on the chore will one day pay off. You will find that your family has budgeted sufficiently to take a vacation, pay for needed repairs on the house, or, at the least, get rid of some of those bills that never seem to go away.

If you find these worksheets helpful, you may want to continue using them on a monthly basis. We recommend that you make your own copies or use a light erasable pencil and make new notations each month.

PART I

Where Your Money Is Now: Current Expenses

The worksheets in this section provide a snapshot of your family's day-to-day finances. You can track your current expenses by jotting down the amount you spend on taxes, insurance, food at home and in restaurants, medical and dental services, and credit card purchases. Later, you can use these sheets to construct a monthly budget and an annual cash-flow statement that will help you make the necessary changes in your spending habits. This will enable you to redirect your income toward your goals.

WORKSHEET 1:
MONTHLY FOOD EXPENSES

Food and other supermarket purchases take a large share of a family's budget, but unless you keep careful track of these expenses for at least a month or more, you won't realize how big a share it is. This monthly worksheet lists four categories of food purchased for home consumption: major weekly supermarket shopping; food purchased occasionally at specialty stores, such as fish, meat, vegetables, and baked goods; extra food purchased during the week; and wine and liquor. (Include products such as paper towels, tissues, and cleaning items under food purchased at supermarkets.) For each week, note how much you spend in each category. At the end of each week, total these amounts and, at the end of the month, add the weekly amounts to get your overall monthly food bill.

Don't be surprised to see fluctuations from week to week and from month to month. Birthdays, holidays, and entertaining can easily increase your food spending.

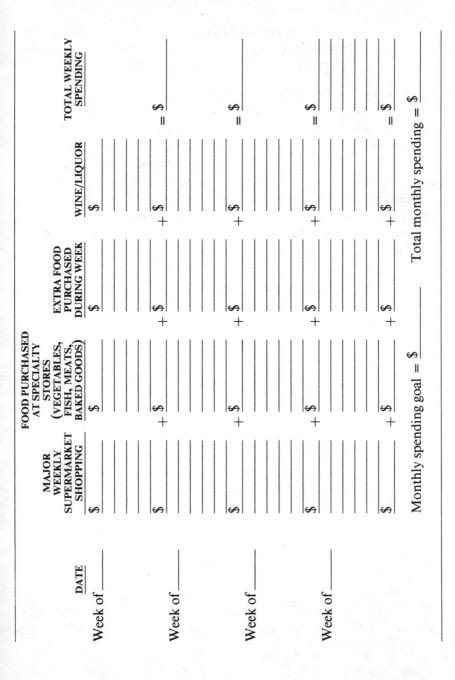

DATE	MAJOR WEEKLY SUPERMARKET SHOPPING		FOOD PURCHASED AT SPECIALTY STORES (VEGETABLES, FISH, MEATS, BAKED GOODS)		EXTRA FOOD PURCHASED DURING WEEK		WINE/LIQUOR		TOTAL WEEKLY SPENDING
Week of ____	$ ___		$ ___		$ ___		$ ___		___
Week of ____	$ ___	+	$ ___	+	$ ___	+	$ ___	=	$ ___
Week of ____	$ ___	+	$ ___	+	$ ___	+	$ ___	=	$ ___
Week of ____	$ ___	+	$ ___	+	$ ___	+	$ ___	=	$ ___
Week of ____	$ ___	+	$ ___	+	$ ___	+	$ ___	=	$ ___

Monthly spending goal = $ _____   Total monthly spending = $ _____

WORKSHEET 2:
HOUSEHOLD MAINTENANCE/
IMPROVEMENT EXPENSES

For many homeowners, household maintenance and repairs are major expenses. This yearly worksheet will help you record these expenses, as well as any major improvements you make. First, list the type of maintenance, such as having the carpets professionally cleaned, or list a major improvement, such as a new hot-water heater or a new roof. Record the date when the work is completed and the total cost of the job. Once you have a record of these expenses for one year, you'll have a good idea of how much you spend annually in this area. A record of these expenses is also vital should you decide to sell your home, as some of these costs add to the *basis* of the property. Basis, a term used for tax purposes, is important because it determines, on the sale of your home, the gain on which you must eventually pay income tax.

YEAR: _____

TYPE OF MAINTENANCE/ IMPROVEMENT	DATE	COST
_____	_____	$ _____
_____	_____	_____
_____	_____	_____
_____	_____	_____
_____	_____	_____
_____	_____	_____
_____	_____	_____
_____	_____	_____
_____	_____	_____
_____	_____	_____
_____	_____	_____
_____	_____	_____
	Total	$ _____

WORKSHEET 3:
MONTHLY CASH SPENDING

This worksheet helps you keep track of your monthly *cash* spending. List the purchase, the date, and the amount. By keeping tabs on these daily cash purchases (ideally for several months, so you may want to duplicate the worksheet), you'll quickly see whether or not you're spending too much on casual spur-of-the-moment purchases. Use this worksheet to record your cash spending for restaurant meals (not for other food expenses), entertainment, and vacation items, as well as any other cash outlays during the month.

YEAR: _____

MONTH: _____

PURCHASE	DATE	AMOUNT PAID
_____	_____	$ _____
_____	_____	_____
_____	_____	_____
_____	_____	_____
_____	_____	_____
_____	_____	_____
_____	_____	_____
_____	_____	_____
_____	_____	_____

Total cash spending $ _____

MONTH: _____

PURCHASE	DATE	AMOUNT PAID
		$ _____

Total cash spending $ _____

WORKSHEET 4:
MONTHLY CREDIT CARD SPENDING

You can record all your monthly purchases made with credit cards on this worksheet. Many families own several credit cards and appreciate the convenience, but their frequent use can be a major drain on the budget. More important, a credit card can transform an ordinary expenditure into a debt, which then becomes nondiscretionary. That is, you no longer have the *choice* of whether or not to buy something but instead have assumed the obligation to repay.

Record each purchase you make with a credit card. (You may list expenses here that you've already recorded on other worksheets.) Note the card used, the item purchased, and the amount charged. Record any restaurant, vacation, travel, and entertainment expense charged on a credit card.

Many families also use the cash advance feature of their credit cards. If you have taken a cash advance, list it under the column for purchases and note the amount. At the end of the month, total the amounts bought with the credit cards.

At the bottom of this worksheet, record and total the monthly finance charges paid on each card and the amount repaid on each account.

This information can help you use credit more wisely. You may find, for example, that you're using your high-cost cards to make expensive purchases that take some time to pay off. If you are, it would be prudent to switch cards, or stop using them altogether. You may also want to repay some accounts in full each month to avoid high finance charges, or you may want to avoid putting a cash advance on an account that you plan to pay in full. You may also decide to stop using credit cards for nontangible items, such as restaurant meals. Duplicate the worksheet if you want to maintain a monthly record of these expenses.

Worksheet 5 will help you keep a record of all your credit cards.

YEAR: _____

MONTH: _____

CREDIT CARD	PURCHASE	AMOUNT CHARGED
		$ _____
_____	_____	_____
_____	_____	_____
_____	_____	_____
_____	_____	_____
_____	_____	_____
_____	_____	_____
_____	_____	_____
_____	_____	_____
	Total credit card spending	$ _____

CREDIT CARD	FINANCE CHARGE PAID FOR THE MONTH	AMOUNT REPAID FOR THE MONTH
_____	$ _____	$ _____
_____	_____	_____
_____	_____	_____
_____	_____	_____
_____	_____	_____
_____	_____	_____
_____	_____	_____
_____	_____	_____
	Total finance charge	$ _____
	Total amount repaid	$ _____

MONTH: _____

CREDIT CARD	PURCHASE	AMOUNT CHARGED
_____	_____	$ _____
_____	_____	_____
_____	_____	_____
_____	_____	_____
_____	_____	_____
_____	_____	_____
_____	_____	_____
_____	_____	_____
	Total credit card spending	$ _____

CREDIT CARD	FINANCE CHARGE PAID FOR THE MONTH	AMOUNT REPAID FOR THE MONTH
_____	$ _____	$ _____
_____	_____	_____
_____	_____	_____
_____	_____	_____
_____	_____	_____
_____	_____	_____
_____	_____	_____
	Total finance charge	$ _____
	Total amount repaid	$ _____

WORKSHEET 5:
CREDIT CARD INFORMATION

For each account, list the name of the card, the account number, the number to call for lost cards, the billing cycle date (the date the account closes for the month), the grace period during which you can pay the balance in full without incurring a finance charge, the annual percentage rate, the annual fee, and the amount of finance charges you paid last year.

This worksheet can help you determine whether you are paying too much in fees or interest and whether you should drop some cards and shop around for new ones offering more favorable terms. By knowing when the billing cycle ends, you can time your purchases to minimize finance charges. If you don't pay off the account in full each month, making a payment at the beginning of the cycle and adding new purchases at the end will lower your finance charges.

CREDIT CARD	ACCOUNT NUMBER	NUMBER TO CALL FOR LOST CARDS	BILLING CYCLE DATE
_____	_____	_____	_____
_____	_____	_____	_____
_____	_____	_____	_____
_____	_____	_____	_____
_____	_____	_____	_____
_____	_____	_____	_____
_____	_____	_____	_____
_____	_____	_____	_____
_____	_____	_____	_____
_____	_____	_____	_____
_____	_____	_____	_____
_____	_____	_____	_____
_____	_____	_____	_____
_____	_____	_____	_____
_____	_____	_____	_____
_____	_____	_____	_____

GRACE PERIOD	ANNUAL PERCENTAGE RATE	ANNUAL FEE	AMOUNT OF FINANCE CHARGE PAID LAST YEAR
_____	_____ %	$ _____	$ _____
_____	_____	_____	_____
_____	_____	_____	_____
_____	_____	_____	_____
_____	_____	_____	_____
_____	_____	_____	_____
_____	_____	_____	_____
_____	_____	_____	_____
_____	_____	_____	_____
_____	_____	_____	_____
_____	_____	_____	_____
_____	_____	_____	_____
_____	_____	_____	_____
_____	_____	_____	_____
_____	_____	_____	_____
_____	_____	_____	_____

WORKSHEET 6:
INSURANCE EXPENDITURES

Insurance is a big budget item for most families. This worksheet helps you become aware of your total insurance expenditures and record important information about your policies.

First, gather all your current policies and recent insurance bills. Record the name of the company that has underwritten each policy (use the exact name that's printed on the policy document). Write in the amount of coverage. For an *automobile policy* you may have several coverages; for example, collision, liability, and uninsured motorist. A *homeowner's policy* may offer the basic coverage as well as additional coverage for liability and loss of use of the property. A *life insurance* policy will have just one coverage, but many families have more than one policy; be sure to include information on all the life insurance policies you own. Next, list the semiannual, quarterly, or monthly payment due dates. Now fill in the amount you owe on each payment due date. In the last column, total the amount you spend annually for each policy, and then total the amount of all your policies.

YEAR: _____

TYPE OF INSURANCE	COMPANY	AMOUNT OF COVERAGE
Automobile	_____	_____
		_____
		_____
		_____
Homeowner's	_____	_____
		_____
Life insurance		
Policy 1 (spouse)	_____	_____
Policy 2 (self)	_____	_____
(List other	_____	_____
policies)	_____	_____
	_____	_____
Health	_____	_____
Disability	_____	_____
Other	_____	_____

PAYMENT DUE DATES	AMOUNT PAID	ANNUAL AMOUNT SPENT
_____	$ _____	
_____	_____	
		$ _____
_____		_____
_____	_____	_____
_____	_____	
_____	_____	
_____	_____	
_____	_____	
_____	_____	
_____	_____	
_____	_____	[1] _____
_____	_____	_____
_____	_____	_____
_____	_____	_____

Total insurance expenditure $ _____

[1] Add premiums for all policies

WORKSHEET 7:
MEDICAL AND DENTAL EXPENSES

This worksheet helps you keep track of the family's medical and dental expenses and of any reimbursements received from insurance carriers.

First, list the services, doctor, and family member who used the service. Fill in the date of the service and the fee, and note whether you've paid it. Next, record the date any insurance claim was submitted to your carrier, the date payment was received, and the total amount received. At the end of the year, total the fees you were charged and the amount reimbursed by insurance companies. Subtract the two amounts to arrive at your total out-of-pocket medical cost for the year—a useful number to have when it's time to prepare tax returns.

YEAR: _____

SERVICE AND DOCTOR	FAMILY MEMBER	DATE OF SERVICE	FEE
			$
		Total fees charged	$

DATE INSURANCE CLAIM SUBMITTED	DATE PAYMENT RECEIVED	AMOUNT RECEIVED
		$

Total amount reimbursed $ _____

Total out-of-pocket expense $ _____

WORKSHEET 8:
TAX EXPENDITURES

Although most people have their taxes automatically deducted from each paycheck, it is useful to know exactly how much of your income goes to taxes each year.

If you make estimated tax payments, you can use this worksheet to record the amounts and dates of those payments. List the total amount you expect to pay in the column labeled *annual amount paid this year.* If you don't make estimated payments, pull together from last year's tax return and W-2 forms the tax amounts you paid, and enter and total them in the last column. Comparing the amounts on the last two columns will tell you if your tax liability is increasing.

YEAR: _____

TYPE OF TAX	PAYMENT DUE DATES[1]
Federal income	_____
	_____
	_____
	_____
	_____
State income	_____
	_____
	_____
	_____
	_____
City income	_____
	_____
	_____
	_____
	_____
Property	_____
	_____
	_____
	_____
	_____
Social Security (FICA)	. . . .

AMOUNT PAID[1]	ANNUAL AMOUNT PAID THIS YEAR[2]	ANNUAL AMOUNT PAID LAST YEAR
$ _____		
_____		
_____		
_____	$ _____	$ _____
$ _____		
_____		
_____	$ _____	$ _____
$ _____		
_____		
_____	$ _____	$ _____
$ _____		
_____		
_____		
_____	$ _____	$ _____
	$ _____	$ _____
Total tax paid	$ _____	$ _____

[1]Give dates and amount of estimated taxes if applicable.
[2]Include all amounts withheld from paycheck.

WORKSHEET 9:
HOLIDAY EXPENSES

Credit counselors agree that the Christmas holidays are often a big drain on family budgets. Many people overspend either because they are enticed by merchants' offers of "no payments until February" or because of their need for psychological gratification. The best way to avoid heavy post-holiday debts is to set a realistic figure for total holiday spending before shopping and *stick to it*. This worksheet is designed to help you do that.

The first column lists the *type* of holiday expenses you are likely to incur. In the next column, list the *estimated* amount you have targeted to spend. In the third column, list the *actual* amount you spent, and in the fourth column, list *how* you paid for the purchase—with cash, a check, or a credit card.

TYPE OF EXPENSE	ESTIMATED EXPENSE
Presents—family	
spouse	$ _____
children	_____
parents	_____
other	_____
Presents—other	
friends	
children's teachers	_____
hairdresser	_____
paperboy/girl	_____
mail carrier	_____
colleagues at work	_____
other	_____
Wrapping paper/ribbon	_____
Cards, including photo expenses	_____
Postage	
cards	_____
packages	_____
Christmas tree	_____
Decorations	_____
Holiday baking	_____
Special restaurant meals	_____
Charities	_____
Other	_____
Total	$ _____

ACTUAL AMOUNT SPENT

HOW PAID? (CASH, CHECK, CREDIT CARD)

$ _____

_____

_____

_____

_____

_____

_____

_____

_____

_____

_____

_____

_____

_____

$

WORKSHEET 10:
MONTHLY CASH FLOW

This summary worksheet helps you ascertain your monthly cash flow; that is, what income is coming in and how it is spent.

In the *monthly income* column, total the gross amounts of all your income, including salary, interest, dividends, pension, annuities, Social Security, and, if applicable, alimony or child support. Fill in the amounts in the categories that apply to you. Think of your monthly expenditures as paycheck deductions, recurring monthly expenditures, or pro-rated expenditures.

Paycheck deductions obviously include taxes but also contributions to savings plans, repayment of loans from a credit union or a 401(k) plan, life and health insurance plans offered by your employer, union dues, and so on.

Recurring expenditures are those expenses your family incurs on a regular basis. They may be the same each month (a mortgage payment, for example) or may vary, such as the amount you pay to decrease a credit card debt. List what you spend monthly for food, gasoline, entertainment (including baby-sitters), utilities, home maintenance, et cetera. Under *mortgage or rent,* be sure to include amounts you repay on equity credit lines, if any. Under *other loan payments,* list amounts repaid on installment loans other than for your car. (Car payment is listed separately.) The total amounts repaid on credit card accounts go in the category *charge account repayments.* If you regularly put a fixed amount into a personal savings account or if you must regularly buy prescription drugs or spend money for medical treatment, list those amounts under recurring expenses. If you make monthly insurance payments, list those in the *other* category.

Many families do not spend money for their insurance, clothing, vacation, or tax needs each month. If this is your situation, the best way to account for these very real expenses is to pro-rate the annual total of these expenses on a monthly basis. Enter one-twelfth of the yearly expenses of these items as a monthly amount. Do the same for any estimated income or property tax payments.

Now total all your monthly expenses. If your expenditures exceed your income, you should reevaluate your spending habits. It's possible that you may be sinking into more debt each month by using credit cards and equity credit lines to cover immediate needs.

MONTHLY INCOME	AMOUNT
Salary	$
spouse	_____
self	_____
Interest	_____
Dividends	_____
Pensions	_____
Annuities	_____
Social Security	_____
Alimony/child support	_____
Other	_____
	_____
	_____
Total monthly income	$ _____

	MONTHLY EXPENSES	**AMOUNT**
Paycheck deductions	Taxes	$ _____
	federal	_____
	state	_____
	local	_____
	Social Security (FICA)	_____
	Contributions to:	
	savings plans	_____
	loan repayment	_____
	health insurance	_____
	life insurance	_____
	union dues	_____
Recurring expenses	Mortgage or rent	_____
	Utilities	
	gas	_____
	electricity	_____
	telephone	_____
	sanitation pickup	_____
	Food	_____
	Car payments	_____
	Gasoline	_____
	Day care or tuition expenses	_____
	Charge account repayments	_____
	Other loan payments	_____
	Personal: laundry/dry cleaning	_____
	Other savings	
	Entertainment	_____
	Children's allowance	_____
	Contributions	_____
	Gifts	_____
	Other	
	prescription drugs	_____
	medical treatment	_____
	household maintenance/	
	improvements	_____
	car maintenance	_____
	other transportation	_____
	other	_____
	Estimated income tax payments	_____
	Property tax payments	_____
Pro-rated expenses	Insurance	_____
	Clothing	_____
	Vacations	_____
	Total monthly expenses	$ _____

WORKSHEET 11:
ANNUAL CASH FLOW

The preceding worksheets, if kept up on a 12-month basis, will furnish you with the necessary information to make a complete accounting of your yearly expenses.

An *annual cash-flow statement* shows you at a glance exactly how much discretionary income you have—that income not committed to paying for essentials such as food, shelter, taxes, child care, and utilities. It will enable you to find room for some reallocation of finances in the amounts spent on discretionary items, such as savings, vacations, entertainment, and, to some extent, food.

YEAR: _____

ANNUAL INCOME

SOURCE	AMOUNT
Salary	
spouse	$ _____
self	_____
Interest	_____
Dividends	_____
Pensions	_____
Annuities	_____
Social Security	_____
Alimony/child support	_____
Other	
(list separately)	_____
	_____
	_____
Total income	$ _____

ANNUAL EXPENDITURES

TYPE	AMOUNT
Taxes	$ _____
Housing	
mortgage	_____
rent	_____
Insurance	_____
Day care	
(school tuition)	_____
Food	_____
Clothing	_____
Utilities	
electricity	_____
gas	_____
water	_____
telephone	_____
other	_____
Car payments	_____
Gasoline	_____
Other transportation	_____
Savings	_____
Vacations	_____
Entertainment	_____
Charge account interest	_____
Home maintenance	_____
Medical: prescription drugs, etc.	_____
Other	_____
Other	_____
Total expenditures	$ _____

PART II

Taking Stock of
Your Family's Finances:
Current Assets

The worksheets in this section can serve as a record of your savings and investment instruments, including those plans offered by your place of employment.

Evaluating these assets can help you pinpoint how much you must set aside for your long-term goals—a new home, an education fund for your children, an early retirement.

WORKSHEET 12:
ASSETS AND INVESTMENTS

List your current savings and investments on this worksheet. Once you know your savings picture, you can make some long-range decisions.

First, gather your most recent account statements (or the instrument itself, as in the case of CDs). Ask the benefits administrator at work for information about your vested pension benefits from either your company's defined-benefit or defined-contribution plan. Although the Employee Retirement Income Security Act (ERISA) entitles you to a statement of those benefits once a year, you have to request it, since employers are not required to provide regular statements. (ERISA does not cover 401[k] plans, a type of defined-contribution plan, but most of these plans do furnish periodic statements to employees.)

If you have a savings account or an investment that isn't included on the worksheet, list it at the bottom. You should also record accounts that are held in your children's names.

Information on the value of your investments should come from the most recent semiannual, quarterly, or monthly statements furnished by the financial institutions. (We recommend that you take an inventory of your savings twice a year to figure out your rate of savings and investment growth or depletion. A good time to take the inventory is when you receive most of your account statements.)

Note the amount in each account and the last time you took inventory. Then list the interest rate (or rate of return) your accounts are earning. If your earnings seem skimpy, you may want to move your money into instruments paying higher rates. If a maturity date is applicable, note that information as well—it's helpful if interest rates suddenly rise and you decide to move your money elsewhere. If, for example, your CDs are earning three percentage points less than competing instruments but the money is locked up for another three years, you'll have to weigh the disadvantage of paying an early withdrawal penalty against the advantage of earning a higher rate.

In the next two columns, note whether the interest earnings are tax-exempt, as in the case of municipal bonds, or tax-deferred, as in the case of cash-value life insurance. Depending on your situation, you may find it's worthwhile for you to shift your assets into tax-favored investments.

In the last column, note the general purpose for each account; for example, emergencies, education, buying a new house or remodeling an old one. Then move on to worksheet 13, which breaks down your savings into more specific categories.

TYPE OF ACCOUNT	WHERE HELD	ACCOUNT NUMBER	AMOUNT IN ACCOUNT
Regular checking	————	————	————
NOW account checking	————	————	————
Bank money market deposit account	————	————	————
Bank savings account	————	————	————
Certificates of deposit			
6-month	————	————	————
1-year	————	————	————
1.5-year	————	————	————
3-year	————	————	————
5-year	————	————	————
other	————	————	————
Credit union savings account	————	————	————
U.S. treasury bills	————	————	————
U.S. treasury bonds	————	————	————
U.S. savings bonds (series EE)	————	————	————
Money market mutual fund	————	————	————
Tax-exempt money market fund	————	————	————
Bond mutual fund	————	————	————
Stock mutual fund	————	————	————
Other mutual funds	————	————	————
Cash value life insurance	————	————	————
Deferred annuities	————	————	————
Defined-contribution plan at work (other than 401[k]) vested balance	————	————	————
401(k) plan	————	————	————
Expected monthly benefit from defined-benefit pension plan at work	————	————	————
Stocks (list separately)	————	————	————
Bonds (list separately)	————	————	————

TYPE OF ACCOUNT	AMOUNT IN ACCOUNT AT LAST INVENTORY	INTEREST RATE OR RATE OF RETURN
Regular checking	_____	_____
NOW account checking	_____	_____
Bank money market deposit account	_____	_____
Bank savings account	_____	_____
Certificates of deposit		
6-month	_____	_____
1-year	_____	_____
1.5-year	_____	_____
3-year	_____	_____
5-year	_____	_____
other	_____	_____
Credit union savings account	_____	_____
U.S. treasury bills	_____	_____
U.S. treasury bonds	_____	_____
U.S. savings bonds (series EE)	_____	_____
Money market mutual fund	_____	_____
Tax-exempt money market fund	_____	_____
Bond mutual fund	_____	_____
Stock mutual fund	_____	_____
Other mutual funds	_____	_____
Cash value life insurance	_____	_____
Deferred annuities	_____	_____
Defined-contribution plan at work (other than 401[k]) vested balance	_____	_____
401(k) plan	_____	_____
Expected monthly benefit from defined-benefit pension plan at work	_____	_____
Stocks (list separately)	_____	_____
Bonds (list separately)	_____	_____

WHEN ACCOUNT MATURES (IF APPLICABLE)	ARE INTEREST EARNINGS TAX-EXEMPT?	ARE INTEREST EARNINGS TAX-DEFERRED?	PURPOSE OF ACCOUNT

WORKSHEET 13:
A BREAKDOWN OF YOUR SAVINGS

Ideally, families should try to establish the following financial resources:

- cash on hand to pay current bills
- emergency funds totaling $10,000 to $15,000 (or six months' income)
- capital funds for large purchases
- education funds for children
- retirement funds

Total the amounts you have set aside for each purpose, using the previously completed worksheets. Money in a checking account or money market fund may be earmarked to pay current bills, and should be totaled in the *cash on hand* slot. Money set aside for a down payment on a house or for a new car is considered *capital funds*. Perhaps the cash value in a universal life insurance policy is reserved for education. Money kept in IRA, Keogh, pension accounts, and deferred annuities is undoubtedly slotted for your retirement.

PURPOSE OF ACCOUNT	AMOUNT IN ACCOUNT	AMOUNT IN ACCOUNT AT LAST INVENTORY
Cash on hand	$ _____	$ _____
Emergency funds	_____	_____
Capital funds	_____	_____
Education funds	_____	_____
Retirement funds	_____	_____

PART III

Where You Want Your Money
to Go: Financial Goals

After assessing how you currently spend your money, you might see a need to change your spending and saving habits. The worksheets in this section can help you clearly define your goals and then reallocate your money to achieve them.

WORKSHEET 14:
YOUR FINANCIAL GOALS

The following worksheet helps define your short-term, intermediate-term, and long-term financial goals.

Short-term goals are generally those you want to accomplish within one year. They may include paying off all your outstanding credit card balances, saving for a vacation, or buying a new stereo system. *Intermediate-term* goals are those that you wish to achieve within two to nine years, such as saving the down payment for a new car or house or accumulating enough cash to replace the roof or the furnace in your home. *Long-term* goals are those that you hope to achieve in 10 or more years, including saving for college costs and retirement.

Whether a particular goal is short-, intermediate-, or long-term depends on where you are in the family life cycle. For a couple in their thirties, saving for retirement is a long-term goal, but a couple in their mid-fifties will view retirement savings as a more immediate goal.

On each worksheet list the goal, the target date for achieving it, the amount needed, the amount you've saved so far, and how you plan to accumulate the balance.

DATE: _____

GOAL	TARGET DATE	AMOUNT NEEDED	AMOUNT SAVED	WAYS TO ACHIEVE GOAL
		$	$	

WORKSHEET 15:
MONTHLY CASH FLOW: SETTING NEW GOALS

This monthly cash-flow worksheet is identical to the one you completed in Part I, but this one is based on *where you would like your money to go* after redefining your spending priorities and setting your new financial goals.

For example, you may be disturbed by the amount you've charged so far to credit card accounts, and you may decide in the future to charge less (and pay less interest) and divert these savings to your company's savings plan. If such is the case, this new cash-flow worksheet would show an increase in your payroll deductions for the company's savings plan. Whereas many of your monthly expenses are fixed, the categories of food, charge account repayment, personal expenses, gifts, contributions, entertainment, and savings should allow room for some adjustments in your spending and saving habits.

And, once you've filled out this worksheet, you can project your new cash flow on an annual basis, using the annual cash-flow worksheet in Part I.

MONTHLY INCOME	AMOUNT
Salary	$
spouse	_____
self	_____
Interest	_____
Dividends	_____
Pensions	_____
Annuities	_____
Social Security	_____
Alimony/child support	_____
Other	_____
	_____
	_____
	_____
Total monthly income	$_____

	MONTHLY EXPENSES	AMOUNT
Paycheck deductions	Taxes	
	federal	$ _____
	state	_____
	local	_____
	Social Security (FICA)	_____
	Contributions to:	
	savings plans	_____
	loan repayment	_____
	health insurance	_____
	life insurance	_____
	union dues	_____
Recurring expenses	Mortgage or rent	_____
	Utilities	
	gas	_____
	electricity	_____
	telephone	_____
	sanitation pickup	_____
	Food	_____
	Car payments	_____
	Gasoline	_____
	Day care or tuition expenses	_____
	Charge account repayments	_____
	Other loan payments	_____
	Personal: laundry/dry cleaning	_____
	Other savings	_____
	Entertainment	_____
	Children's allowance	_____
	Contributions	_____
	Gifts	_____
	Other	
	prescription drugs	_____
	medical treatment	_____
	household maintenance/	
	improvements	_____
	other transportation	_____
	other	_____
	Estimated income tax payments	_____
	Property tax payments	_____
Pro-rated expenses	Insurance	_____
	Clothing	_____
	Vacations	_____
	Total monthly expenses	$ _____

WORKSHEET 16:
A MONTHLY BUDGET: SETTING NEW GOALS

After you've filled out the hypothetical monthly cash-flow worksheet, it's time to tackle the job of allocating or budgeting your monthly income. *Budgeting is essential if you are to realize your financial goals.* If your hypothetical cash-flow worksheets show that you need to spend less for food and divert more to savings, this monthly budget (if followed closely) will pinpoint where the changes should occur.

At the top of the worksheet, fill in the net amount of your paycheck for each pay period, whether paid weekly or on a bimonthly basis. At the beginning of each pay period list the amount from each paycheck that you must set aside for various fixed expenditures—utilities, mortgage payments, food, loan repayment, and so on. Then allocate money to discretionary items—entertainment, gifts, some food.

Credit cards are listed under *charge account repayment* and under *miscellaneous spending;* the amount you wish to spend in repayment reflects what you've spent in the past. Your cash spending and amounts charged during the month can also be considered current miscellaneous spending. If you don't pay your entire credit card balances by their due dates, the unpaid amounts charged this month will show up in subsequent months as debts. As you will see, controlling the amounts spent for credit card purchases may be the real secret to achieving your financial goals.

Next, list the amounts you have allocated to various prorated expenses. For example, you may want to reserve $50 from each paycheck to pay quarterly insurance premiums. Simply deposit it in a checking-savings account or a money market account until the bill comes due. Do the same for clothing purchases, vacations, and tax payments.

Unless you believe in deficit spending, the amount budgeted, as well as the amount spent, should equal or be less than the net amount of your paycheck. If both amounts regularly exceed your net pay, you may be slowly building a burden of debt that could make it difficult to achieve all your financial goals. Again, examine the amounts you are charging. If they regularly exceed the amount you are able to pay back each month, that is a red flag indicating that your financial structure is shaky and needs a new foundation based on controlled expenditures and savings.

You may want to make extra copies of this worksheet so you can keep track of your budget on a yearly basis.

MONTH: _____

| | EXPENSES | PAY PERIOD 1 $ _____ | |
		AMOUNT BUDGETED	AMOUNT SPENT
	Mortgage/rent	$ _____	$ _____
	Utilities		
	gas	_____	_____
	electricity	_____	_____
	telephone	_____	_____
	garbage	_____	_____
Recurring expenses	Food		
	at home	_____	_____
	in restaurants	_____	_____
	Car payment	_____	_____
	Gasoline	_____	_____
	Day care/tuition	_____	_____
	Charge account repayment (list cards)		
	_____	_____	_____
	_____	_____	_____
	_____	_____	_____
	_____	_____	_____
	_____	_____	_____
	Other loan payments	_____	_____
	Personal: laundry/dry cleaning	_____	_____
	Savings	_____	_____
	Entertainment, baby-sitter	_____	_____
	Allowances	_____	_____
	Gifts/contributions	_____	_____
	Miscellaneous spending		
	cash	_____	_____
	credit cards	_____	_____
	Other	_____	_____
	Estimated income tax payments	_____	_____
Pro-rated expenses	Property tax payments	_____	_____
	Insurance	_____	_____
	Clothing	_____	_____
	Vacations	_____	_____
	Other	_____	_____
	Total	$ _____	$ _____
	Shortfall or Excess		$ _____

| | EXPENSES | PAY PERIOD 2 $ _____ | |
		AMOUNT BUDGETED	AMOUNT SPENT
	Mortgage/rent	$ _____	$ _____
	Utilities		
	gas	_____	_____
	electricity	_____	_____
	telephone	_____	_____
	garbage	_____	_____
Recurring expenses	Food		
	at home	_____	_____
	in restaurants	_____	_____
	Car payment	_____	_____
	Gasoline	_____	_____
	Day care/tuition	_____	_____
	Charge account repayment (list cards)		
	_____	_____	_____
	_____	_____	_____
	_____	_____	_____
	_____	_____	_____
	_____	_____	_____
	Other loan payments	_____	_____
	Personal: laundry/dry cleaning	_____	_____
	Savings	_____	_____
	Entertainment, baby-sitter	_____	_____
	Allowances	_____	_____
	Gifts/contributions	_____	_____
	Miscellaneous spending		
	cash	_____	_____
	credit cards	_____	_____
	Other	_____	_____
	Estimated income tax payments	_____	_____
Pro-rated expenses	Property tax payments	_____	_____
	Insurance	_____	_____
	Clothing	_____	_____
	Vacations	_____	_____
	Other	_____	_____
	Total	$ _____	$ _____
	Shortfall or Excess		$ _____

PAY PERIOD 3 $_____		PAY PERIOD 4 $_____	
AMOUNT BUDGETED	AMOUNT SPENT	AMOUNT BUDGETED	AMOUNT SPENT
$_____	$_____	$_____	$_____
_____	_____	_____	_____
_____	_____	_____	_____
_____	_____	_____	_____
_____	_____	_____	_____
_____	_____	_____	_____
_____	_____	_____	_____
_____	_____	_____	_____
_____	_____	_____	_____
_____	_____	_____	_____
_____	_____	_____	_____
_____	_____	_____	_____
_____	_____	_____	_____
_____	_____	_____	_____
_____	_____	_____	_____
_____	_____	_____	_____
_____	_____	_____	_____
_____	_____	_____	_____
_____	_____	_____	_____
_____	_____	_____	_____
_____	_____	_____	_____
_____	_____	_____	_____
_____	_____	_____	_____
_____	_____	_____	_____
_____	_____	_____	_____
$_____	$_____	$_____	$_____
Shortfall or Excess	$_____	Shortfall or Excess	$_____

Index